To Carol
When ↑
you realize He is all you
need.

Diane Pretty

God
is in the
Details

Diane Pretty

Order this book online at www.trafford.com/07-2316
or email orders@trafford.com

Most Trafford titles are also available at major online book retailers.

© Copyright 2008 Diane Pretty.
All rights reserved. No part of this publication may be reproduced, stored in a retrieval system, or transmitted, in any form or by any means, electronic, mechanical, photocopying, recording, or otherwise, without the written prior permission of the author.

Note for Librarians: A cataloguing record for this book is available from Library and Archives Canada at www.collectionscanada.ca/amicus/index-e.html

Printed in Victoria, BC, Canada.

ISBN: 978-1-4251-5264-2

We at Trafford believe that it is the responsibility of us all, as both individuals and corporations, to make choices that are environmentally and socially sound. You, in turn, are supporting this responsible conduct each time you purchase a Trafford book, or make use of our publishing services. To find out how you are helping, please visit www.trafford.com/responsiblepublishing.html

Our mission is to efficiently provide the world's finest, most comprehensive book publishing service, enabling every author to experience success. To find out how to publish your book, your way, and have it available worldwide, visit us online at www.trafford.com/10510

 www.trafford.com

North America & international
toll-free: 1 888 232 4444 (USA & Canada)
phone: 250 383 6864 ♦ fax: 250 383 6804 ♦ email: info@trafford.com

The United Kingdom & Europe
phone: +44 (0)1865 722 113 ♦ local rate: 0845 230 9601
facsimile: +44 (0)1865 722 868 ♦ email: info.uk@trafford.com

10 9 8 7 6 5 4 3

Help Me, Holy Spirit
By Glenda Fulton Davis

"I want to talk like Jesus, words of truth my mouth to speak.
I want to walk like Jesus, circumspect with holy feet.
I want to see like Jesus, through the man into the heart.
I want to be like Jesus, Spirit-filled and set apart.
I want to live like Jesus, faithful to my God above.
I want to give like Jesus, not of duty, but of love.
I want to pray like Jesus, "Father, not my will but thine."
I want to stay like Jesus, in God's presence all the time.
I want to dare like Jesus, speaking out on wrong and sin.
I want to care like Jesus, seeking souls to win for Him.
I want to preach like Jesus, seeing captive souls set free.
I want to teach of Jesus, of the blood He shed for me.
0 help me, Holy Spirit, live the way I want to live.
0 help me, Holy Spirit, learn the meaning of forgive.
Lift me up to things above, that through me all may see
Christ and His redeeming love exemplified in me."

DEDICATION

To my husband, George, whom I will always consider the true hero of my book! I am also dedicating my story to cancer patients everywhere; for those who have survived, and for those who are still fighting their battle. I pray that one day there will be a cure, but until then, never give up hope!

ACKNOWLEDGMENTS

⋅⋅ ⊷❦⊶ ⋅⋅

UNIVERSITY OF TEXAS, MD ANDERSON CANCER CLINIC, HOUSTON , TX
You are rated NUMBER ONE for a reason.

DR. FREDRICK HAGEMEISTER, MD PROFESSOR OF MEDICINE, DEPARTMENT OF LYMPHOMA/ MYELOMA, UNIVERSITY OF TEXAS, MD ANDERSON CANCER CLINIC.
George and I could never thank you enough for all the excellent care you gave him during his treatments at MD Anderson. In our eyes, there is no better doctor anywhere. We love you, Dr H!

AMYE MOSHIER, PA
Amye, you are the BEST! Dr H had better know that he has the best Physician's Assistant he could have. You have always been the one that I could count on when no one

else could help. You are a valuable part of the Lymphoma team and we will never forget you.

DR. ROSS REUL, MD DIRECTOR OF SURGICAL INNOVATIONS, ST. LUKE'S EPISCOPAL HOSPITAL AND THE TEXAS HEART INSTITUTE, HOUSTON, TX
Our many thanks to you for the marvelous job you did during George's bypass surgery. Forgive me for thinking you were just a "kid"; you are a fine doctor!

DR. MARCIA LIEPMAN, MD MEDICAL ONCOLOGIST, WEST MICHIGAN CANCER CENTER, KALAMAZOO, MI
Dr. Liepman is our local Oncologist who is taking great care of George at this time.

DR. LISA BOOTH, MD BOOTH MEDICAL CENTER, HOWE, IN
Thank you Dr. Booth for all the excellent care you give both George and I. We always know that we are in good hands and we appreciate the fact that if you don't have the answers, you find someone who does!

PASTOR JOHN SHOUP CHURCH OF THE NAZARENE, STURGIS, MI
Our love and heartfelt "thank you" for all the years you have spent as our spiritual leader. We simply cannot say enough good things about you. We know that there are some pastors who go "beyond the call of duty" but you exceeded even that when you made that trip to Houston to be with us during George's surgery. Thank you, Pastor, for everything.

ELLEN CHRISTOPHER
It was because of you that I finally decided that I would write this book. You have been an inspiration to me for many years

God is in the Details

and I want to thank you for that. We miss you at church, but I hope you are right where God has planted you! I love you.

BRAD, JUDI AND RADAR (Our dear "Texas friends")
Thank you so much for being true friends to me when I was alone and needed someone. Brad, thank you for all the conversations we had when we took those pups for a walk. Judi, I hope your journey through cancer is over! You are brave and have fought a good fight, and God willing you too have received your "miracle." Radar, Buddy misses you!

OUR CHURCH FAMILY (Sturgis Church of the Nazarene)
I have no words to express our gratitude for your love, support, and for the many prayers that you have offered on our behalf. You have been faithful through it all! I look forward to many more years of worshiping with all of you. You truly are our "family."

DIANE MOSHIER
Little did either of us know when I brought you that little book that I would be thanking you for the title for my own book! You don't have a clue how many times I looked at that magnet and remembered that God really does care about every detail in our lives. Thank you so much!

NANCY BERKLUND
I will forever be grateful to you for that phone call! You gave me that extra "push" in the right direction; between you and God we made our way to MD Anderson. Thank you also for all your support while we were in Houston. George and I both enjoyed our time together with both you and Rondi. Our prayers continue for Rondi that God will give her many years to share with her family.

Diane Pretty

SUSAN SNOWDEN, EDITOR @
www.snowdeneditorial.com

COVER DESIGN BY MIKE BENNETT @
www.mikebennettgraphics.com

INTRODUCTION

·· ❧ ··

Life really seemed to be coming full circle for us. It was the beginning of March, 2004, and George and I were looking forward to spring in Michigan. It had been a long, hard winter for us. My dad had been seriously ill for a couple of years and we had been caring for him around the clock for the past several months. It was a job that we had taken on both willingly and lovingly, but nonetheless, caretaking had become our entire life. We weren't able to leave Dad alone for any length of time and our social life had become nonexistent. We were both looking forward to some "normalcy" once again.

Months earlier, George had asked me to take a look at his neck just behind his right ear. He had noticed some lumps and wondered what they were. I thought they were probably swollen glands so we both dismissed it as that. We were so busy caring for my dad that I put it completely out of my mind.

One day shortly after Dad passed away, George brought

them to my attention again. I was surprised that they were still there and when I felt around on his neck, I could tell that they were larger than before. I had never known swollen glands to last so long and just to be on the safe side, we made an appointment with our family doctor to have them checked.

When George got home from the appointment, I met him at the door, anxious to hear what the doctor had to say. "She's scheduling an appointment for me to see an ENT." (Ear, nose, and throat doctor) At this point I was still not too concerned. In my mind I thought it was probably an inflammation of some kind and we would find out for sure once he saw the ENT.

The day of that appointment came and George was going alone. I had made plans prior to this appointment and I thought I could trust him to handle this by himself. (Why I thought that I will never know!) When he came home the first question I asked was, "Well, what did he say?" In his nonchalant manner he mentioned, "He's going to do a biopsy." *That got my attention!* "A biopsy? What does he expect to find?" I had a dozen questions, but of course, George had none of the answers. He *never* asked the questions that I would have asked and by now I had decided that this was the *last* time he would go to the doctor alone!

A few days later we went to Lutheran Hospital in Fort Wayne, for this little outpatient surgery. I was sitting in the waiting room and had barely started to read the book I had brought with me before the doctor was finished and they were calling me back to the recovery room. The doctor was already there waiting to talk to me. He told us that he had removed the largest of the nodes and was sending them to pathology. The report would be back in just a few days and his office would call us with the results. He said, "I don't see any *red flags*, so I don't expect this to be anything

God is in the Details

to worry about." I asked him what he thought it might be but he really had no idea. He had never seen anything like it but said it could have been some sort of inflammation that had gone untreated. (That's what I thought too at the time.) He wasn't worried, so why should we be?

George was still feeling the effects of the sedation so he slept all the way home. I was listening to the radio and had already put this little "adventure" out of my mind. (Or so I thought.)

Once we got home, I decided to go online and see what I could find out about swollen glands. The more I thought about it, the more I wondered what could cause them to last for months. The word that kept jumping out at me was lymphoma. "This can't be lymphoma," I thought. "The doctor said it's probably nothing to worry about." As I read along, I found some information that caused me to really become alarmed. It said, "You should be concerned if the lumps are hard, rubbery, without pain, getting bigger, and not going away!" If that didn't describe those lumps on George's neck, nothing did!

I finally decided to get off the computer and stop reading about lymphoma. I was just making myself more upset and I needed to wait until the doctor's office called.

I wasn't able to put it out of my mind, no matter how hard I tried to keep busy. Just when I thought I would go nuts waiting for the doctor's office to call, *the phone rang*. The voice that I heard on the other end was that of the doctor himself! He was calling *personally* to speak to George. I heard him pick up the extension and decided not to hang up because I wanted to hear what the doctor had to say.

One

·· ✿ ··

"The report came back and you have non-Hodgkin's lymphoma." All the breath went out of me in that instant. All I could think of was all the things that I had read on the Internet. This doctor just told us that George has *cancer*. I couldn't believe it. I didn't want to hear him say those words; I wanted to run away to a safe place and not have to deal with this. "Had he really used the word *lymphoma*?" I knew people that had been diagnosed with lymphoma and they had died. "Had this doctor just handed George a death sentence?" I tried to listen to everything he was saying so that I would be able to "process" it all in my mind. He was saying that it appeared to be of the malt cell type but that he had sent the biopsy slides to Mayo Clinic for a second opinion. I had no idea that lymphoma was classified into different types. Oh, I knew there was Hodgkin's and non-Hodgkin's but that was as much as I knew at that point. "We should hear back from Mayo in about a week and someone will call you then." That was it;

God is in the Details

that was the end of the conversation. I was standing there in the kitchen and I knew that George would be walking in at any moment asking, "What's lymphoma?"

I was right; those were the first words out of his mouth. All I could tell him was what little I knew. "It's a form of cancer of the lymph glands." What else could I say? I really didn't know much more than that. I knew he had a million questions, as I did. I told him that I was going to the computer and see what else I could find and I promised him that I would come back with the information and we would talk about it.

I can't even begin to tell you how many emotions ran through me when I left that kitchen. I know that most people who hear a diagnosis of cancer feel that same knot of fear twisting inside of them, just as I had when I heard that word. Why is it that a single word can strike such fear within us? I believe it's the fear of the unknown, the fear that all the horror stories we have heard about cancer are about to come true, and we fear losing someone we love.

I went into my office and started searching everything I could find. I knew that non-Hodgkin's lymphoma was the worst kind to have. I read and read; I searched until I had all the information I could find. I already felt a lot better. I had learned that malt cell was considered to be an indolent (low-grade) form of lymphoma. It is one of the milder forms and 77 percent of people who have it have a survival of more than ten years. "OK, this is something we can deal with and George will be just fine." I had finally stopped shaking and took a deep breath and went to search for George to tell him the good news. I told him everything that I had just learned and all we needed to do now was find an oncologist who specialized in lymphoma.

Although things seemed to be on a more positive note, I couldn't ignore the fact that we were still dealing with cancer. I was sure there would be some kind of treatment that George would have to go through and that made my heart sink. I couldn't believe any of this was happening to us. Cancer happens to *other* people, not my husband.

We managed to have a couple of good days while I was beginning to look for oncologists in our area. We were living in that space of time where we were able to find our comfort zone while putting off making decisions about anything. I think both George and I were trying to adjust to this new information that I had found and, honestly, things didn't seem so bad at all. Yes George had cancer, but we were hopeful. *Then the second phone call came.*

I certainly didn't expect to hear the doctor's voice again. As was the case the time before, once I heard his voice, that feeling of dread reappeared. He told me that he just read the report from Mayo Clinic and that they didn't agree with the first opinion.

It's absolutely amazing how thoughts can go through your mind so fast. One second I was thinking that there might be no lymphoma after all; the next second I was wondering if the news was worse than we were told to begin with. My mind went back and forth until the doctor began speaking again. I sensed from the tone in his voice that this was not good news. He went on to say that Mayo's pathologist said that it was lymphoma, but not the malt cell. They were sure it was something called mantle cell.

He asked whether or not we wanted him to refer George to an oncologist in the Fort Wayne area. I didn't know *what* I wanted at the time, but I knew that I did *not* want to hear what he was telling me. He suggested that I discuss this with George and give him a call back to let him know what we decided to do. *Mantle cell lymphoma*; I had never heard of it. Back to the computer I went.

During my research I was becoming astounded to learn just how many varieties and types of non-Hodgkin's lymphoma there were. One website claimed there were at

God is in the Details

least forty while other sites claimed there were even more than that. All I knew was that with this new information, I felt that our luck had run out and that a death sentence was in George's future for sure.

The very first thing I read about MCL, as it's called, is that it is highly aggressive and resistant to treatment. The prognosis was not good. The article went on the say that there were really no treatments that offered much hope at that time. I went on reading anything and everything I could find in a desperate attempt to prove all those other articles wrong. I found that it is a relatively rare form of B-cell lymphoma, a type of non-Hodgkin's lymphoma that is a cancer of the blood. Each year in the United States, approximately fourteen hundred people are diagnosed with MCL. The incidence of this type of cancer varies in different countries. It appears to be more common in people who are Caucasian or of European descent.

Lymphomas are cancers that begin in lymphocytes, a type of white blood cell that is an important part of our infection fighting immune system. The lymphocytes are found mainly in lymph nodes as well as in other parts of the body that make up the immune system, such as the spleen or the bone marrow. One of the first signs of MCL can be swelling in the neck, armpit, or groin. Although there are exceptions, people who are diagnosed with MCL are usually older adults and for some unknown reason it also tends to occur more often in men than in women. Generally the cancer is not confined to one area. It occurs in one or more lymph nodes but at the same time can also appear in the digestive system, lungs, bone marrow, skin, or spleen. More times than not, MCL had spread by the time it is diagnosed by a doctor.

This wasn't good, any of it. I was more convinced than ever that this was the worst possible diagnosis we could have had as far as lymphoma was concerned. I went back to my computer and tried to find chat groups of people who had MCL. Everything I found only caused me more grief. I tried talking to George about some of the things I had learned, but I really don't think he followed most of it. He had never been one to read a lot and do research so I knew this was going to be up to me. It had become my *quest* to find as much information as possible so that when questions needed to be asked, I would be educated enough to know exactly which ones to ask. All I was going to get from George was silence. His way of dealing with things that he didn't want to face was to withdraw and not talk. I expected it, but what I wanted was for him to take an active part in all this. I could already tell that wasn't going to happen, at least not now.

I needed to find a doctor who knew enough about MCL to give us the best hope as far as prognosis and treatment were concerned. I thought about calling Mayo Clinic since that's where the actual diagnosis came from. I made a call and was surprised that I was able to get an appointment in about three weeks. We talked about it and George said he would go anywhere I decided. After rethinking it, I asked him if he thought we should start somewhere closer to home. He didn't care, so I was left to make that decision.

I called the University of Michigan after that to see what information I could find about their oncology department. The receptionist told me that they had doctors who treated a lot of lymphoma patients so I booked an appointment. I was thrilled when she said we could see a doctor in two weeks! George was happy to have the appointment closer to home, and my next step was to call and cancel the one at Mayo Clinic. Finally, I felt like I had made a step in the right direction and now all we had to do was to wait for two weeks.

I can't tell you that waiting was easy. *It was not.* I kept myself busy reading and making lists of questions for the

God is in the Details

oncologist at U of M. I made a trip to Fort Wayne to get records and reports to carry with us when we went. I kept reading articles anywhere I could find one to read, and so far I came up with nothing positive. Everything I read just brought more "doom and gloom." All I could think of was, "I'm not ready to lose my husband!"

George spent his time keeping his feelings to himself. Anytime I would ask him if he was worried he would tell me "No." Once in a while he would let his guard down and would tell me that he was concerned that if anything should happen, he wanted to make sure I was taken care of. I know he trusted God with his future, and so did I, but I will admit I was scared to death. I was afraid to let myself think too far past the moment.

If our lives weren't already turned completely upside down, add to that the fact that our whole backyard was completely torn up. We had to have a new septic system installed. The bulldozers had been digging for days now. The entire yard was one huge pile of dirt, all my flower beds had been destroyed, and the poor dogs had no yard to play in. We constructed a makeshift fence of sorts in one corner so that they would have a place to go "potty," but beyond that, it was total chaos.

I hadn't known at the time we had contracted to do all this that we would be dealing with our latest news. I have to say, however, that it really put it all into perspective for me. For days I had been complaining about the mess in the yard. I had been grieving the loss of my beautiful flowers, and I had been very impatient about the fact that the dogs didn't have their yard. *Sometimes it takes a big boulder to hit us in the face just to get our attention!*

I had just met that big attention getter in the form of cancer. I could already see what lay ahead with the backyard…it was all planned out. First the septic system would go in, next the sprinklers, then the grass, and finally the new deck. *How simple that all seemed now.* How mundane and small. All of a sudden, out of nowhere, everything in my life had changed. There was no "schedule." we didn't have a set of plans all mapped out for our life anymore. Neither the noise of the bulldozers nor the inconvenience of not having a yard in perfect order was a priority to me. *My husband had cancer, incurable cancer, rare, aggressive, and resistant to treatment.* God had really gotten my attention in a big way. I had gotten all caught up again in "things," I had wanted my life to be full of things that I could control, things that had a plan and that met *my* timeline. I didn't want this interruption in my life! Well guess what? *Nobody is ever ready for cancer!* I had wanted my life back after my dad passed away. I wanted some time to be free, time to breathe, and time to enjoy life once again. It looked as if none of that was to happen for me.

The day of our appointment at U of M finally arrived and we were on our way. *"Ready or not."* I had spent two weeks trying to prepare for this day but I realized I still wasn't ready to hear what they might say. How is it possible to prepare for the unknown?

We walked into the hospital hand in hand, neither of us in the mood to talk. We were taken into an exam room by a physician's assistant, who took all the information and had George change into a gown. She came back in, did a brief exam, and asked us to wait there until the doctor was ready for us. The whole atmosphere seemed so formal and cold to me.

The doctor came in and introduced himself and took a few minutes to review all the information we had just given the PA. He checked George over, felt around for any more swollen glands, and then told us that he would be doing a bone marrow biopsy. I was expecting that, but my heart still dropped to the floor. I knew what George was in for so I was more than a little relieved when the doctor

God is in the Details

asked me to leave the room.

I went to a small waiting area until the procedure was over. As I was sitting there, I was thinking about what I had read about bone marrow biopsies. I knew what was about to take place just down the hall and I was glad that George had no clue!

The area of George's back would be numbed; then the doctor or an assistant was going to place a special type of needle through the skin in George's back, just below his waist and into the bone itself. The needle is about half as thick as a pencil and has a handle on the end that the doctor holds. The needle is moved into the bone by a twisting motion, much like a corkscrew would be moved through a cork. When the needle passes through the top layer of bone, the doctor uses a syringe to pull a liquid sample of bone marrow through the needle. After the liquid is removed, the doctor carefully moves the needle farther into the bone itself and takes a solid sample of the marrow. This is called a core biopsy. Once the needle is removed, pressure is applied and a bandage is placed over the area. This procedure is necessary for the *staging* to find out if the lymphoma has infiltrated the bone marrow. I had learned all this from my research and as I sat there I was wondering why I always felt it necessary to know quite so much.

I didn't want to think; I couldn't focus on anything except getting out of there and going home. I didn't want to be there, and most of all, I didn't want my husband to have to go through any of this. I wanted to be anywhere but where I was at that particular moment.

When they came out to tell me I could go back in, I found George dressed and sitting in a chair. I asked him if it had been painful and he said, "Not really, it was more like pressure or a dull ache." That's my George, the brave one who never complains about pain. I hadn't realized how shaken I really was until I sat down in a chair to wait for the doctor to return. I had always been very strong anytime I had been ill or had surgery, but this time I wasn't the patient; I was the spouse. I have to say, at least for me, it was easier being the patient. I felt more in control that way and now all I could do was shake inside. I was unable to do anything about any of this. It was a very unfamiliar feeling to me to see George as the patient this time. *I didn't like it.*

When the doctor came back, he explained that after the biopsy report was completed, the oncology department, along with radiology, would have a meeting to discuss all of George's tests and together they would make a determination as to how to proceed. They would also have a pathologist from U of M look at the pathology slides and he would give his opinion on the diagnosis as well. The doctor told us that he would personally phone us at home on Friday to give us their findings.

More waiting, and to tell the truth, it wasn't getting any easier. A million thoughts went through my head on a daily basis. I always ended up on the computer trying to find something new that I hadn't read before, anything to give me comfort. That didn't happen, for no matter what I read, it all ended up the same. There was no cure for MCL and no one offered us any hope. The feeling of dread was becoming my constant companion.

On the way home that day, we stopped for lunch. Surprisingly, we did enjoy the meal and were able to talk for the first time in what seemed to be a very long time. We even laughed a little about George losing his hair if they decided to do chemotherapy. When I told him that he would lose *all* of his body hair, his comical side surfaced and he made the comment, "Maybe I'll lose these nose hairs along with the rest of my hair." (He hates nose hair!) It felt wonderful to laugh. I had felt so tense for so long and now I could feel that tension easing and I couldn't believe that we were *actually* laughing.

God is in the Details

We had to pass by a place that sold flags on the way home. George had always talked about wanting an American flag in our yard but had never wanted to spend the money for one. That day we stopped and looked around and he decided that he was going to buy one. He looked at every size flag they had and also at the flag poles they carried. He picked out a pole with an eagle on the top and ordered the size flag he wanted. They would be delivering it in a couple of weeks and would install it in our front yard. I was so happy that he was finally getting his flag, until it hit me. *He was getting his flag because he thought he was going to die.* I felt that my heart was going to break into a million pieces. So much for the lighthearted afternoon and the laughter we had just shared. There was nothing lighthearted about cancer.

I couldn't help but think about all the struggles we had during our marriage, all the years when I had yearned for a closer relationship, more communication, more time spent doing things together. Now, none of that seemed important. I didn't know how long we had together, whether there would be a future or not for us. In the blink of an eye, our lives had changed forever. It was never going to be the same again

Friday came and just as promised, the call came. The diagnosis was really mantle cell lymphoma. I waited to hear when chemo would begin, but instead, I got a few moments of silence. The doctor told me that basically they were at a loss as to how to approach it. They couldn't actually *agree* on a treatment. He did say that they rarely, if ever, saw MCL in an early stage or without organ involvement, but according to all of the tests, they could only find the lymphoma in his neck. There was no bone marrow involvement either so they classified George as having Stage 1, meaning it hadn't spread past the original site. Since he had no symptoms, he was considered I-A. Symptoms being chills, unexplained fever, night sweats, weight loss, or fatigue. What the doctor suggested was what he called a "wait and see" approach. He said he would see us in a month for a follow-up and go from there. I have to say that the relief was sweet. I felt a huge weight lift from my shoulders. I know now that I was just living in denial; nevertheless, *I welcomed it.* When I look back, I think God was giving us time to rest before we had to meet the biggest challenge of our lives

George's energy level seemed to stay the same; he never felt sick at all, and for now life went on. The yard was done, the deck was built, and the new flag was proudly flying in our front yard. Right then life seemed good. No symptoms was a "good thing" and I could almost get used to living in this denial...*Almost.* I say almost because when I least expected it, the full reality would hit me once again. Friends and family were wonderful, but try as I may, all I could feel was fear and that awful dread of what was ahead of us whenever I would allow myself to *think.*

It was the end of June before we were able to get our next appointment, but the time had come and we were on our way to see what, if anything, had changed since our last visit.

When we got there, the oncologist read over his notes and felt around on George's neck. "The lymph nodes in the neck are still about the same," he said. He continued feeling around to the front of his neck and the next thing I heard was "The node near his clavicle seems a bit smaller." *What node near the clavicle?* This was the first we had heard of another node. All we knew about were the nodes on the back of his neck. He said George was still Stage II. I was totally shocked, "What did he mean, Stage II?" I said, "You told us Stage I when we saw you the first time!" He had no reply. None. He just continued feeling around on George's body, looking for swollen lymph nodes, and I sat in the chair wondering what I was supposed to say now. Finally I asked him why he was telling us Stage II. He said that since the nodes were in two locations, the staging would be that of Stage II.

God is in the Details

I was totally confused by that time. When I started to question him further, he became very vague and never gave me a straight answer. I was beginning to think that he didn't really remember *what* he had said to us during the previous appointment. "How could he possibly remember how lymph nodes felt on a particular person two months ago?" Surely he must have felt a lot of lymph nodes in that amount of time. I couldn't help but wonder if the cancer had spread and he didn't want to tell us, or if there had actually been a clavicle node all along. None of it made a bit of sense to me, but I waited to see what would follow. He went on to say that everything looked "good" and that he would see us in three months. We would continue with this "wait and see" approach until that time.

Now I am not usually at a loss for words, but somehow I couldn't find anything else to say. I was in shock to put it simply. We had been told Stage I and now we were being told Stage II. I asked about treatment and he said he wasn't recommending any treatment at that time. His last remark before we left the room was this. "I know it's hard living with uncertainty, but that's easier than living with chemotherapy." That was it. That was the end of the visit. Now we could go home, live in denial for another three months, and return again for a follow-up.

George was very upbeat and relieved on the way home. He had escaped hearing anything about treatments and all he could think of was that he was "free" for another three months. I was quiet on the ride home this time. Thoughts were running through my head and all I could do was remember the things that I had read online about MCL. I tried to get to the place where George was living, that place that he always goes to when there are things he doesn't want to face. The place of denial, the comfort zone, where nothing is real at that moment. *But this was real.* I tried so hard, but it wouldn't work for me. My time of denial was

24

Diane Pretty

over and I couldn't get past the fact that this doctor based his opinion to wait for three long months on a simple exam where he did *nothing* more than feel the lumps on George's neck and clavicle. It didn't add up. Nothing about the visit made sense at all. "Why were there no tests run this time, no CT scans, nothing?" Weren't tests and scans the way doctors followed the progress of cancers? My mind refused to allow me to retreat from reality this time.

When we got home I was still unable to stop thinking about all that had happened...or perhaps all that had *not* happened at the doctor that day.

I found some information about MD Anderson Cancer Clinic in Houston and began to read in earnest about their approach to MCL. I had discovered that this type of lymphoma can be aggressive, but in most cases it was considered indolent (that word again) meaning low grade, slow growing. I could almost see the reasoning behind a "wait and see" approach since this type of lymphoma was thought to be indolent and why rush to treatment if everything was staying in control? I decided to phone MD Anderson and get some information.

I placed the call and asked a few questions about their facility and about making an appointment there. They told me that they needed to see George's records first and once they were reviewed, they would call and set up an appointment if we wanted one. I just knew that what we needed was a *second opinion*.

I got the ball rolling. It was on July 2 that I made that first call to MD Anderson, but the following week I ran into a snag. I couldn't get the records sent to Houston until the pathology slides were released. After more waiting, more phone calls, red tape and lack of communication between parties, things finally began falling into place. Exactly three weeks after I placed that first call, I got a call back from MD Anderson. This was the call that was to change the direction

God is in the Details

in which we had been going. We had an appointment in Houston if we wanted it…*and I wanted it desperately.* (Now all I had to do was convince George that we were going twelve hundred miles for another opinion.)

The nurse at MD Anderson told me in no uncertain terms that they did NOT agree with U of M's "wait and see" approach for George's diagnosis. I had never been comfortable with that opinion, but at the same time I wasn't anxious for George to go through chemo either. I do know that I was ready for someone to take time to explain things to us and give us some other options.

Who is to ever say what path is the right path? No one can know that for sure and certainly no doctor has all the answers, but I needed some peace or at least some assurance that the current approach was reasonable. I had just been told that it wasn't.

Now, how was I to go about convincing George? I already knew he wasn't going to like my latest plan. I finally told him what I had done and I could already see that I was right, *he wasn't happy.* His first comment was, "It's too far away." I had anticipated that attitude and tried to think of something to say to convince him. I tried to make him see my logic, but he was set on staying home and living in denial for another three months.

Finally I knew what I needed to say. I simply said to him, "What if something happens to you and I knew that if I could have said something to convince you to go to Houston, we might have had a different outcome?" Then I added, "Would you want me to have to live with that the rest of my life?" Long story short…we were on a plane for Houston two days later.

Two

·· ❦ ··

Wednesday, July 28, brought us to Houston. We arrived late in the day and checked into the hotel. We had an early appointment the next morning so our first day in Texas ended with an early bedtime. Some of the fear and anxiety that I had felt in previous months had suddenly been replaced by excitement. *I was excited to be there.* I had already come to think of MD Anderson as the answer to my prayers.

I had done my fair share of praying during this time, but I must say that God felt very far away from me. I had been a Christian for thirty years and had gone through some very difficult times, but accepting that my husband could die from cancer had shaken my faith to its very core. This had sent me to a spot very deep within myself in order to discover what I believed about God and His grace. I wasn't questioning God exactly, but myself, and just how much I was ready to submit this all to His control. I have always had a control issue. I am not comfortable when I can't somehow

27

God is in the Details

contribute to the outcome of things. I could already see that this was definitely something that I could not control, and in fact, no one could. What I would do about it and how I would handle it would remain to be seen.

There had been an incident that happened at the exact time I was trying to decide whether or not we should actually come to Houston. I had been praying and asking God for direction and in my mind I thought that this was the place He wanted us to be. What happened next only made me more certain than ever that God's hand really was in this.

Nancy Berklund called me from Minnesota. She had been a neighbor of ours and had moved to Minnesota years earlier. I hadn't heard from Nancy since she left Michigan. Someone who knew us both had told Nancy about George having cancer. When she called me out of the blue, I was surprised. The reason for her call was to see how George was doing, but mainly to urge me to take him to MD Anderson in Houston! Her daughter Rondi had been going there for treatment for brain cancer. She had been seen by other doctors but none of them held out much hope for her. She had had surgery to remove as much of the cancer as possible but all they would tell her was that they couldn't do much else for her. Nancy had taken her to MD Anderson and had gotten a much different opinion. Rondi was still going to Houston every two months for tests and was doing well. They had given her the hope of seeing her young children grow up. Nancy couldn't stop talking about what a wonderful place it was and finally said, "Just don't take no for an answer, get him there as soon as possible." Coincidence? I really don't believe in coincidence. *I knew then and I still know today, that this was only the beginning of the works of God that I would see during our journey.*

Our first morning in Houston had arrived and we were headed for our first appointment of the day. The size of the University of Texas Medical Center Complex totally amazed both George and me. We had never seen so many medical buildings and hospitals in one place before. MD Anderson itself was enormous. Lucky for us there were signs and people everywhere to direct us. We were about to begin the first of several long days there.

First we met with a woman who was in charge of new patients. We filled out page after page after page of information before we were able to go to the next appointment. George had been asked by the research department if he would participate in their ongoing lymphoma research at MDA by consenting to have extra vials of blood taken each time he went to the lab, as well as tissue samples if he had to have procedures done. Neither of us had ever thought about anything like that, but we were happy to be able to contribute anything we could to help find a cure. Little did George know at the time just how much blood he was going to have to have drawn during his stay in Houston, but that extra vial wasn't too much to ask for the good it could possibly do. The first blood draw was next on the list. *It had already started.*

After that we met with the doctor who had been assigned to our case. He was one of sixteen doctors on staff in the lymphoma–myeloma department. We knew from our first meeting that he was a brilliant doctor, but he seemed to be lacking a bit in "bedside manner." His name is Dr. Fredrick Hagemeister or Dr H as we soon began calling him. (Our first impression that he was a brilliant doctor was correct; the part about his bedside manner changed as we got to know him!) We met with him for about an hour and a half during which time he talked and we listened.

He started by telling us that by reviewing the records we had sent, it appeared that George did, in fact, have MCL. He didn't mince any words as he began telling us what we could expect if he should recommend treatment and if

God is in the Details

we decided to have it done at MDA. He told us about the prognosis for MCL, about the previous treatments that had not been very successful, and then he told us about the MD Anderson protocol. It was a fairly new treatment and so far was the most promising treatment they had for this type of lymphoma. He said that the treatment is called R-Hyper C-VAD and that it is a complex and intensive combination of a number of anti-cancer drugs. Cycle A would be given in treatments 1, 3, and 5 and another treatment of drugs called ARA-C would be given as Cycle B treatments 2, 4, and 6. George would receive six rounds of chemo over a period of six to eight months and the treatments would require a hospital stay each time. Cycle A would require a four to five-day stay and Cycle B about three days. He was going to order a round of tests including more blood tests, CT scans, a PET scan, as well as a colonoscopy and EGD where they would take numerous blind biopsies of the tissues in the gastric tract. George would be having another bone marrow biopsy as well.

Dr H said he wanted a complete picture before he would actually make a final diagnosis and advise treatment. In his opinion though, regardless of the staging of MCL, this type of lymphoma can begin as indolent and become aggressive without warning and there was no way he would ever suggest a "wait and see" approach. At least now we had one of the things I had been searching for. We had the assurance that we would get all the options explained to us and from there we would be able to make an informed decision. I had made the right decision to get a second opinion.

When we left the office that day, I felt overwhelmed by all the information we were presented with. I hated that George had to go through so many tests; I hated the fact that we had to go all the way to Texas to get the information that we so desperately wanted, and I hated

Diane Pretty

that once again my life was interrupted. I was so tired and I already suspected that this was only the beginning of what was to come.

The testing had begun. George had appointments scheduled one after another for days. While we waited at the various departments, we started talking about the "What if's." What if Dr H suggests that George have treatment now? What if he wants him to come to Houston to have it done? What if we decided that's what we needed to do? We would need a place to live for six to nine months or possibly longer. Where do you even begin to find a place to live in just a few short days? We would need a place where we could bring our three dogs, a place that would rent to us without a long-term lease, and, of course, somewhere close to the hospital. Dr H had told us specifically that he wanted us to be within ten to fifteen minutes of the hospital. That alone limited our choices. If I thought that life was moving faster than I preferred, *it had just picked up speed.*

Saturday and Sunday were free days. There were no appointments scheduled so I called a realtor and told her our situation and what we would need if we found ourselves in Houston for the long haul. She wasn't encouraging. First of all, rentals in Houston were very expensive. The rentals in the medical center area were difficult to come by unless we wanted to rent an apartment. Short-term rentals were all but impossible to find and the fact that we had three dogs didn't help matters.

We found some lovely apartments which would allow pets, *two pets*, we had three! Even with two dogs I couldn't imagine trying to walk them both several times every day. That seemed like an awful lot of extra work to me.

We found an adorable house in just the right place, they would allow our dogs, and *we wanted it*. It was perfect and I fell in love with it the minute I saw it. It had a great fenced-in yard, which meant no dog walking for me. I

God is in the Details

could already imagine living there. I knew we still had to find out for sure if George was going to have chemo, but I was already certain he was. I asked the realtor to see if we could rent the house and she promised to call us as soon as she knew anything. We waited for a couple of hours on pins and needles before she called. She had to tell us that it was already rented. "Well, back to square one," I told myself. Obviously that one wasn't meant for us.

After two days of searching newspapers and calling leads, I hit a brick wall. Now what would we do? I was forgetting a little saying that I had written down in so many places, hidden away until the time I happened across it just when I needed it most. It goes like this, "If God brings you to it, He will bring you through it." (I had just found it written in the back of my checkbook.) Time to take a deep breath. If we were supposed to live in Houston, then we would find a place to accommodate us and all three dogs.

Monday came and we were once again back at the hospital for tests. It was relentless and I knew that George was exhausted each time we got back to our room. He wasn't able to go through tests like that every day and have the energy to look for a place to live as well. I decided that I wouldn't bother him with details and would just continue looking on my own.

The next day while he was at the hospital, I rented a car and just drove in each direction until I was about fifteen minutes from the hospital. At that point I would head back the way I came and drive street by street looking for "For Rent" signs. Every time I saw a sign I would pull over and write down the phone number. By the time I got back to the hospital I had two pages of numbers to call. Every single person that I talked to turned me down. I decided to buy a newspaper and try that approach. More of the same. Nobody wanted to rent a house to us without at least a one-year lease,

32

and most of them wouldn't even consider three dogs.

I noticed one listing that was very vague. There was no mention of pets, it didn't say anything about a lease, and it was five minutes from the medical center. That was the first thing that caught my attention. I immediately called the number listed in the ad. A gentleman answered the phone and I asked about the house he had for rent. The first thing he said was that he required a one-year lease. I started to say "Thank you" and hang up, but something stopped me. (Maybe it was that little notation that I had discovered written in the back of my checkbook.) I got a bit bolder and asked him if I could explain my situation to him. He seemed hesitant at first so I just kept talking. In the end he actually listened to my plight and gave me an address and told me to drive by it and see if it was something I thought would suit my needs.

The house wasn't hard to find, and he was right, it was just about five minutes from the hospital. I drove into the driveway and peeked in the window. It looked like a nice house inside although I wasn't "in love" with the outside like I had been with the other house we had found. I had to remind myself that we weren't *buying* it after all; we just needed to rent it for awhile. The neighborhood looked old and established and was very clean. That was something that appealed to me since I would be spending a lot of time there alone. I decided that if the owner would rent it to us, then I wanted it. He was to meet us there the following morning before George was scheduled for his first appointment.

We arrived at the house the next morning around ten. Once inside I knew that this was the house for us. The owner said he would rent the house to us for six months with the option of staying longer if we needed to. To make it even more appealing, we didn't have to decide on the spot. He knew we still had to talk to the doctor first and

God is in the Details

if we decided then that we would be moving to Houston, the house was ours. *Thank you, God.*

The next day while George was having a PET scan, I made my way to my favorite place in the hospital. It's called "The Park" and it's quiet and tranquil. It's filled with comfy chairs that are separated in a way that you can be alone with your thoughts or sit near someone and have a conversation. There are potted trees growing up in the center of the area, even though it's totally enclosed. The ceiling is about two stories high and at the top it's all glass. There are flowers in planters sitting everywhere; the whole atmosphere is that of being outside in a *real* park. It was the perfect spot for me to go when I had serious planning to do.

There's a cute little gift shop located in the same area as well as a Starbuck's. That particular day, I decided to get my favorite drink, a chai latte. I pulled up a chair, propped up my feet, and took out my notebook. That poor notebook was looking pretty ragged these day. I had been taking plenty of notes over the past few months. I was afraid to leave anything to memory, so once again I took out my pen and found a clean page.

Along with page after page of medical notes, I had begun writing notes regarding the move to Houston if that should become a reality. We would need to rent furniture and today that was on the top of my list of things to check on. I had to find a washer and dryer and was hoping I could find those to rent along with the furniture. I had already checked on utilities, phone, and cable TV and had the phone numbers written down. I had even gotten the name of the man who did lawn work at the house we were hoping to rent. I knew that I had to take care of all these details and allow George to think of nothing else but getting ready for the battle of his life.

I sat there thinking about a lot of things. Mostly I was

wondering how George was going to deal with all this. He had always been so healthy and I knew that this had taken him by surprise. I knew he was going to do his best to keep a positive attitude and get through the chemo the best way he could. I wasn't sure that he really had the full knowledge of what was in store for him, so I knew that I had to do everything I could to keep his focus on getting well. George deals best with things as they come and doesn't like to plan too far ahead. I sometimes wish that I had that luxury, but someone has to be the planner and organizer and I guess that's me. George much prefers his "cave." That's where he visits often when he doesn't want to be bothered. (I got that term from a marriage book I had read years ago.) That term suits George so well.

I hated the thought of leaving home and moving to Houston, even though it would be temporary. I would be leaving my family and everything that I held near and dear. I would be totally alone and totally responsible for taking care of every minute detail as well as caring for George's physical needs. Was I up to the task? I wasn't sure, but I knew that I would find the strength as I needed it. We hadn't planned for any of this to happen, but we found ourselves here and all we could do was to take it a day at a time.

One of the reasons I felt we needed to be in Houston for the treatments was that George needed to be away from all the distractions that he would find at home. If we were home, he would be trying to work. The phone would be ringing off the hook and he would be trying to deal with customers or people who wanted to call and "chat." I knew that he didn't need all that going on while he wasn't really well enough to handle it. I knew George only too well, and I knew that's exactly what he would be doing. This was one more reason why he needed me to be the strong one and take over. He knew I was capable and now all I needed to do was convince myself of that.

God is in the Details

By the end of the week, all the tests were completed but our appointment to meet back with Dr H had been postponed. We had to wait until the following week so we decided to fly back home. We were so exhausted, both physically and mentally and the thought of being in our own bed at night was almost more joy than we could handle!

We had a few more things to accomplish before we could leave. We found a store where we could rent furniture, so we headed over there to see what we could find. We spent about an hour picking out the things we thought we would need, including the washer and dryer that I was hoping to find. They agreed to keep everything "on hold" for us until we called them the following week. I was pleased with all that I had accomplished in such a short time, and that notebook of mine was overflowing!

Three

·· ❧ ··

On the flight home I started thinking about all the people I had seen at MDA. It occurred to me that we weren't in this battle alone. I had met people with the same fears that I had. I had never been around so many people with cancer before. I guess that's what I should have expected when we went to a "cancer center," but it had really overwhelmed me. Everywhere I went I was looking into the eyes of cancer patients or their loved ones. I couldn't get away from this disease. In the elevators we would see men with bald heads, women in hats or scarves, and the truly brave ones who didn't bother trying to hide the fact that their hair had been lost to chemotherapy. There were wheelchairs everywhere, people walking the halls pushing their IV poles with medications being pumped into them, sunken faces, frail bodies, people wearing masks because their blood counts were dangerously low from their chemo. At first, I saw it as a scary place, a place that I wouldn't have chosen to visit and a place that I couldn't wait to leave.

37

God is in the Details

I said "at first" because I was beginning to see it in an entirely different light.

I was beginning to see how George coped with the unknown. I knew he must have had his moments when fear gripped him, but he never shared that with me. I couldn't help but wonder what went through his mind when he looked at those same people that I saw. Did he wonder as I did about how many of them would live and how many would die? I knew he couldn't help but wonder about a lot of those things, but he handled this the same way he handled everything else. He kept it inside.

I needed to talk. I spent countless hours feeling so alone that I almost lost hope at times. I thought he was wrong for not sharing those feeling with me. Sometimes I got so angry I wanted to scream at him. I wanted to say to him, "Look this way for once and see ME! I'm scared and I'm hurting and I need you." (But I never did either.) I came to realize that by sharing his feelings and concerns with me, George thought he was adding to my stress. He didn't understand that he was wrong, so that was how he handled it. He thought he had to be strong; I just wanted him to be human. I needed to see that he too was vulnerable. I wanted to be comforted and I needed to comfort him. It wasn't about to happen. George dealt with things in his own way, and *cancer wasn't about to change that part of him.*

Our time at home went too fast. We didn't have a lot of time to talk about the upcoming doctor visit that was only a couple of days away. I had been thinking about what we were going to hear and in my heart I already knew the answer. The doctor was going to tell us that George has MCL and that he needed to come to Houston for treatment. I knew it and I was getting prepared.

We had decided that George should fly back to Houston alone to see the doctor and find out what would happen next. I knew he wasn't going to ask all the right questions and I also knew that he wasn't going to remember everything the doctor told him. He left for Houston with a list of questions that he promised me he would ask, along with a mini tape recorder so that he could record the whole conversation. There was NO way that I was sending him to Houston unarmed. I needed to know what was said and I wanted the *details*.

I was packing boxes to take to Houston. I wanted to have everything ready to go if the doctor said he was ready to start treatments. I packed everything that I knew I couldn't live without, which turned out to be enough to fill a U-Haul from front to back and from top to bottom!! I wanted to take the whole house, but I knew George would have a fit if I did. There were pictures of our family that had to go, regardless. I knew that I would need to look at those on a daily basis so that I could remember all the love that would be waiting for us when we came home again.

Our son James was going to drive my SUV and pull the trailer. I knew that I would never make it if I had to drive. The driving part was easy; it was the U-Haul that was the problem. I had gone to have a hitch installed and to pick up the trailer in a town about forty-five minutes from our house. That was one experience that I never want to repeat. I had taken my friend Betty with me and promised to take her to dinner if she would go along for the ride. I thought I had it mastered until we came out of the restaurant and discovered that someone had blocked me in where I had parked. That called for a major maneuver and a lot of backing up. I was praying that no one I knew was anywhere around to witness my lack of ability when it came to figuring out how to back up my SUV and that U-Haul and make everything go in the same direction. I finally got out of the parking lot and was headed for home. At that point I was thankful that the road was straight and that there was no reason that I would have to back up again.

God is in the Details

George called me as soon as his doctor's appointment was over. "I do have MCL." (We now had three opinions and two were in agreement.) There was none found in the bone marrow or in any organs, which came as a huge surprise to Dr H. He was very happy with those tests results. He advised starting chemotherapy right away and said that he expected excellent results. He told George that in the past, remissions had lasted only as long as eighteen months, but with the newest treatment he was seeing remissions lasting five years and longer. I'm sure that if all he could have promised us was an eighteen month remission, George would have opted not to have treatment, but if we could have five years or longer then we would take it! Although we would have preferred for Dr H to use the word "cure," we knew that MCL remains a non-curable form of lymphoma. I was thanking God for getting us to Houston and for the HOPE that we now had. Things were better than we had first expected! Chemo was scheduled for the following Wednesday, which was August 18.

My son and I, along with the three dogs, left Michigan on Friday the thirteenth! If that wasn't tempting fate or defying superstition, nothing was. The trip went well and we were delighted to find out that the dogs were all excellent travelers. I had spent five days deciding what to take with me and had it all packed and ready when my son arrived at our house. We started out about noon that first day and decided to stop for the night once we found a motel that would allow three dogs. I hadn't really thought about the possibility that we would have such a hard time finding a room. That was one little "item" that wasn't included in my little notebook. Finding that room was no small accomplishment; we must have stopped ten times before we found it. We ended up paying ten dollars extra for *each* dog. We did get an unexpected bonus however! *The cockroaches that came with the room were almost as big as one*

40

of the dogs. The only good thing about that night was the fact that we had a place to sleep. The dogs weren't even anxious to find a spot on the floor, and by morning, I had all three of them in bed with me.

The trip went fast. We made the twelve hundred mile trip to Houston in thirty hours (including the few hours of sleep we had). We were even able to get into the house when we arrived on Saturday night, even though we were a day earlier than we expected.

We had quite a first night in the house. We had NO furniture yet. That was to be delivered on Monday, so we had to make do with whatever we could find in the U-Haul. I brought one air mattress and two blankets. James ended up on the air mattress and I slept on the floor on the blankets. The dogs lucked out…they each had their own bed to sleep on. I have to confess that more than once during the night, I eyed those nice thick dog beds and more than once the idea crossed my mind that maybe they might share their beds with me just as I had shared mine with them the night before!

George was still at his hotel. He had gotten sick the day before and had wound up spending a night in the ER. He was running a temperature and they decided to keep him overnight since he was starting chemo in just a few days. We decided that he should stay there for another night since there was no place for him to sleep at the house.

On Monday morning our son left for the airport and George and I waited for the furniture to be delivered. It arrived on time and was set up for us in no time at all. I even managed to have the washer and dryer installed at the same time. The electricity was on and our phone was hooked up on the same day. We had everything except gas.

The gas company said they wouldn't have anyone out until Tuesday to turn on our gas. In the meantime, we didn't have any hot water! To complicate matters, we had to be at the hospital early on Tuesday morning in order for

God is in the Details

George to have blood work that he needed for his admission to the hospital on Wednesday. We had no choice but to leave on time, and of course, by the time we got back, we had missed the gas man. We found a note on our front door saying that since the gas had been shut off for such a long time, they would need a city permit before they could turn it back on. (The owner of the house had been having a lot of remodeling done to the house so I assumed that was why the gas had been shut off.) I called the number that was listed on the note and spoke to someone in charge of inspections. They told me that the landlord would have to give his OK before they would come out to do the inspection. The landlord was out of town, so now what? I called his cell phone and left him a message. We didn't hear from him for over an hour, but when he called he had already spoken to the inspector. Now all we had to do was wait for the inspection.

They were sending an inspector out right away, so I relaxed, thinking that all was well. Once the inspector arrived and started looking through the house, he informed us that we needed a plumber! It seemed that there were a couple of minor things that needed to be brought up to code. This had nothing to do with getting our gas turned on, but we could do nothing until the *entire* inspection was finished. He would go no further until the plumbing work was done.

I had no idea how to find a plumber in Houston! I opened the phone book only to find page after page of plumbers listed. I looked at the street names and the phone numbers but had no clue where any of them were located. Heck, I didn't even know the name of the street next to ours! I had no idea what side of Houston we were even in! I knew the phone book wasn't the answer.

I called the landlord again and this time he answered on the first try. He said he would call a guy that had done work for him before and ask him if he could come right away. The plumber was there in less than an hour and in just a few minutes, his work was done. All we needed now was a quick inspection and we could get our gas on. All I could think of was, "We are going to have hot water."

The inspector was nice enough to come back the same day, and in a matter of five minutes we had the signed inspection in our hand and now we could call the gas company again. I quickly called them only to be told that they weren't making any more calls for the rest of the day. They would come out the next day between 8 and 5. *We had to be at the hospital the next day.* No amount of explaining about appointments or chemotherapy made a bit of difference. It was their policy to take calls in the order in which they were received and they made no exceptions. So for now, we had no gas, which meant we still had no hot water. We had been in the house for three days now and I was tired of heating water in the microwave just to be able to wash my hair! I kept telling myself that it would only be *one more day.* I recalled an old saying that went like this: "What doesn't kill you makes you stronger" (gotta love those old sayings). I had the feeling that I was going to be very strong in no time.

We had to be at the hospital early on Wednesday to have the CVC (central venous catheter) inserted that would be used to infuse the chemo directly into a large vein in George's chest, just above his heart. I was sitting in the waiting room feeling queasy. We had just watched a video on the whole process and I was ready to give up and say, "Let's just not do this," but that amazing guy just walked in and did what was necessary. When I saw him come back through the door after the procedure, I was amazed by his whole attitude. *He's about the strongest guy I know.* He told me that he makes the better patient and that I make the better caregiver; that's why he has cancer and

God is in the Details

not me. Up until then I would have argued with him but after seeing what he had already gone through, *I think he had a point.* He told me that he could go through just about anything because he had one terrific nurse (me). I wasn't as convinced as he seemed to be. I had so many doubts about all the weeks and months ahead. I wasn't sure I was going to be able to do my part, but I didn't have a choice. We were there for however long it took and there was no place I would be except by his side.

We went to x-ray after that so that they could make sure that the tip of the catheter was in the right spot. Everything was perfect and now all we had to do was wait until they had his bed ready. Back home we went to wait for the gas man.

This time we hadn't missed him but when he did arrive, he said that he still couldn't turn on our gas. He had turned it on briefly but had found a leak right at the meter and now he would have to replace the meter itself. I already knew what that meant...one more day with no gas, one more day without hot water. This time I couldn't remember a single "old saying" that fit the situation. The thoughts I did have weren't for publication.

The hospital called at five to say that George's bed was ready. Off we went to the hospital. (Chemo was beginning but I wasn't ready.)

George was admitted to a room on the ninth floor which is the lymphoma section. *Did I mention that this room didn't look like any hospital room I had ever seen?* It looked more like an upscale hotel. All of the rooms are private. I suppose that's because the patients are all so ill. (Or maybe it was the price of the room!) The beds have controls for everything you could want, right at your fingertips. The beds have air mattresses that patients can adjust to their individual comfort. Each room has a phone, TV, VCR with movies that are brought to the room on a daily basis, and if you can believe this, you can even set the temperature in the room by a simple phone call. There are two menus in the room, one for the patient and one for a guest. All the meals are ordered by phone and are delivered within forty-five minutes by "room service." I would be able to have meals with George anytime I wanted to just by ordering from the guest menu. There was a charge of course for my meals, but the prices were more than reasonable. Everything was immaculate. As we looked around we could almost forget that this was actually a hospital room where chemo would begin in a short time.

My stomach was in that same knot that I was becoming accustomed to carrying around with me. I got George settled into bed and almost immediately someone came in to draw blood. The blood test was necessary before any of the chemo could begin. We were surprised when they took blood from the catheter tube in his chest. They told us they could do that whenever he was in the hospital as long as there was no chemo infusion being administered. George thought that was a great idea. He was already tired of being "poked" from the endless blood tests. Every time he turned around, someone wanted more blood! All we had to do now was wait for the report to come back from the lab.

The first drug was to be Rituximab, or Rituxin as it's usually called. We had been told to expect this to be a rough night for George. There were a lot of side effects to this drug, especially for the first five or six hours. I was prepared to stay with him until the worst was over. George would require constant monitoring during this infusion and just knowing that did nothing to alleviate my stress. I was so worried that something was going to happen to him. I knew that people had actually died from the effects of this drug and no matter how hard I tried, I couldn't get that out of my mind.

I had come to think of chemo as a process where a

God is in the Details

drug brings a person as close to death as possible and then attempts are made to bring them back, this time without cancer. I knew that was a bizarre way of thinking about it, but the more time I spent around cancer patients, the more I realized it wasn't too far from the truth.

What choice did we have at this point? We knew that eventually George would die without treatment. No one knew how long he could live *with* treatment, but he was ready to begin and I had no choice but to support him in any way I could. I didn't envy him, but I respected him for having the determination to go through it. I admit, I was terrified. I needed strength that I didn't have. I was trying my best to trust God to supply that strength, but my fear had taken over and that trust left me for a moment. "Is it possible to say you trust God and at the same time experience this intense fear?" I wondered. *Absolutely and without a doubt I believe that it is.* We are only human after all and the fear of the unknown is a natural thing. I believe that God understands our fear. Ultimately it's what we allow that fear to do to our faith that matters. If we didn't have fear, we wouldn't need God's grace.

We found ourselves waiting again. They had told us they would be bringing in the medication shortly and now that we were prepared for it to begin, we had to wonder what was taking so much time. Just then the nurse came in. "We need consent papers from your doctor and we can't find any," she said. Since it was after hours and the doctors had all gone home, there would be NO chemo tonight. I was so shocked I could barely speak. "How could this be?" We had gotten ourselves prepared and now we had to wait through the whole night. I couldn't believe this, I felt like someone had just played a cruel joke on us. I looked at George and could see how disappointed he was, but I also saw relief. *Maybe he wasn't as ready as I thought he was.* Obviously I wasn't going to spend the night at the

46

hospital so I decided to go on home. George said he just wanted to try to get some sleep; tomorrow would come soon enough.

"Was God preparing us for a lesson in patience as well as a test of faith?" That's the only reason that made sense to me. I could see that nothing in this journey was going to be carved in stone and that we both needed to learn that at the very beginning. I tried to remind myself that life is full of these annoyances and disappointments and that no matter how upset it made me, I wasn't the one in control. I kissed George good night and went home to spend the first night of many, alone with the dogs in a new place.

The next morning I called the hospital to see how the night had gone for George. He was in a very good mood and said that he had spent a comfortable night. Of course he had to rub it in by telling me, "I just had a nice hot shower." I was jealous! We still had no hot water at the house. I had heated water at 7 a.m. in order to wash my hair again. I told George that I would be there as soon as the gas man arrived and got the gas turned on.

About 9 a.m. the gas man showed up only to tell me that he had an emergency on the next block and had to take care of that before he would be able to get to me. *More waiting. More patience required!* This wasn't going to be easy on me. Patience was never my strongest asset and already mine was wearing thin. I called George again to see if they had been able to start the Rituxin. "Not yet." I really wanted to be with him during those first few hours and there I sat, waiting for the gas man.

If I wasn't already on stress overload, one of the dogs was sick. *She was our baby.* A beautiful white American Eskimo named Annie, who was the smartest and sweetest dog in the world. I was really worried about her, but with everything else happening, I hadn't had time to find a vet in Houston. I called around while I was waiting and actually

God is in the Details

found someone who could see her that very afternoon. I was torn between being with George and getting Annie to the vet. I made another call to George to see what he wanted me to do. He said to go ahead and take Annie to the vet because chemo was still on hold.

Somewhere in the midst of all my phone calls, the gas man was ringing the door bell. I had never been so happy to see anyone in my life! (Not really, but it sure seemed like it right then!) I told him that I needed to leave for about an hour and asked him how long he would be. He told me that most of his work would be outside and all he would need to do was to come inside to light all the pilot lights and make sure there were no leaks. He assured me that I would be back in time for him to do that.

Another quick phone call to George before I was ready to leave. *Chemo had started fifteen minutes ago.* "God give me strength" was all I could say as I rushed out the door.

I knew that Annie was ill, but I had no idea just how serious it was. The vet had suspected a problem so he did x-rays. He came back into the room, put the x-rays in the light box, and pointed to a spot at the top of her nose. He told me that she had cancer of her nasal sinuses. That explained her symptoms, but I still couldn't believe this. First George and now our dog. I wasn't prepared for this but he went on to say that he would refer me to a veterinary oncologist if I wanted him to. He said he could get me an appointment for the following day. "How was I going to keep that appointment and be with George at the same time?" I was at the end of my rope. Nothing in my life was going right and there I stood holding my dog and crying a bucket of tears.

Just as I got home, the gas man walked in to say that the meter had been changed and that in a matter of minutes all the pilot lights would be on. He was true to his word and was finished in no time. I was left alone to decide what I was going to do about Annie.

I still needed to be at the hospital with George and I was already dreading the first question he would ask me when I got there. He would ask about Annie. "How am I going to tell him that our dog is dying?" He didn't need this right now. He had all he could manage with chemo and the side effects and now he had to hear this news. Funny how the hot water had been so important only hours ago, and to be honest, I didn't care if we ever had hot water. All I wanted was to go home and have my life the way it used to be.

I finally got to the hospital around 2:30. I felt so bad that I hadn't been there earlier and the feeling of dread hit me about the time I walked into the room. He looked awful and I could tell that he had been having a rough time. The nurse told me that they had stopped the infusion a couple of times because the side effects were so severe. George had a temperature and chills that shook his entire bed. That feeling of complete helplessness flooded me. I knew there was nothing I could do or say to him, so I just walked to his bed and held him. "I'm here now" was all I could think of to say.

I realized that I had been praying ever since I stepped out of the elevator. It seemed that I was always in communication with God these days in some way or another. With everything that was going through my mind, most of the time my prayers were short and to the point. All I needed to say was "God help us" and I knew He was doing just that.

After a while, the shaking stopped and George was able to open his eyes and look at me. I was trying hard not to let him see a reaction out of me, and I was also trying to avoid talking about Annie. The nurse came in and started the infusion again and said he was almost done with the Rituxin and then things should calm down a lot.

The question finally came. "How's Annie? What did

God is in the Details

the vet say?" I was hoping that he wouldn't ask, but I knew he would. I was surprised that I could hold myself together as well as I did when I told him what I had learned. He was quiet. I knew he was trying not to cry and I knew that he wasn't going to talk about it right then. I needed to allow him the space he needed so I just walked over to a chair and sat down.

The Rituxin was finished around six. That was the last of the chemo until the next morning. They were going to give George a chance to recover from the first drug and would only be giving him fluids in his IV overnight. He told me that I should go home and check on Annie and to call him before I went to bed.

When I got home, Annie wouldn't eat. She looked so sad and it broke my heart to look at her. It was as though she knew she was going to leave me. She would always lie in the living room every evening and look out the large windows that stretched from floor to ceiling. All three dogs had their beds in front of those windows and they loved watching people walk by in the hope of seeing a dog or two that they could bark at. *But not this night.* She wouldn't leave my side. Her sweet little face would look at me, her eyes full of questions. She didn't deserve this. She was the best dog anyone could ever have and I was going to lose her.

How much loss was I supposed to bear? I looked at the other two dogs just then. Smokey was an old dog that had belonged to my dad. She was feeble and hadn't made the move to Houston too well. She had a lot of health problems and had become really difficult to deal with. I wondered why it couldn't have been her that was dying instead of our Annie.

I called our kids before I went to bed. I still hadn't gotten used to the two hour time difference and almost didn't call because it had gotten so late. I wanted to tell them that their dad had gotten through the first day of chemo and even though it had been rough, he was doing much better. Then I had to break the news about Annie. It seemed as though all I had done lately was give them bad news. I knew they were all anxious about everything going on in Houston and were very worried about their dad *and* me. I tried not to let them know just how lonesome I was and ended the conversation while I could still pull it off.

After I hung up with the kids, I called George. He was tired from the effects of chemo and I could tell he was depressed. He was heartbroken over Annie and was trying hard not to break down on the phone. I knew he had lain there all evening after I left and thought about her. We talked a little and then the damn broke loose. We cried together until there were no more tears. I had needed him to cry with me, but I didn't expect it. This time he didn't hold it all inside; he gave me what I needed without even realizing it.

I went to bed thinking about the appointment the vet had made for Annie the next day. I wasn't sure whether I wanted to go or not. I knew there wasn't much they could do for her other than very invasive surgery and perhaps some kind of chemo. The vet had been up front with me and told me that all I could expect, even if I put her through all that, was a few months at best. I had to really think more about it before I made my final decision.

By morning, I had decided to call my vet in Michigan. I needed her input on the situation with Annie. When I talked to her she told me that she had lost her basset hound to the same cancer as Annie had. She discouraged me from putting her through surgery because there was really no hope for her. It would be painful for Annie and extremely expensive for me. She told me to give her some over the counter antihistamines that would help with the swelling inside her nose and that would help to make it easier for her to breathe. She told me to call her anytime that I needed

God is in the Details

to talk and she would try to help me though this. Before I hung up, I asked her how I would know when the time came to make the decision to have her put to sleep. She said "You'll just know, Annie will tell you."

I had my answer. I called and canceled the appointment for Annie. I wasn't going to cause her to suffer just because I didn't want her to leave me. I wasn't going to try to keep her alive for a few short months so that I would have her a while longer. I was going to do the best thing I could do for Annie. I would wait until she told me herself that the time had come. "Please, God, help me when it's time to make that decision."

I had been journaling ever since George's diagnosis. I had intended to write about our experiences in dealing with cancer but little did I know that my journals would fill up so quickly. Our life was no longer just about our journey through cancer, but a walk toward something greater. It was becoming a walk in faith.

Four

·· ❦ ··

It was August 20 and the second day of chemo. I was at the hospital before ten. George was feeling much better than he had the night before so we decided to take a walk. Dr. H had told George that he needed to walk as much as possible and we found the area laid out very well for doing just that. We were able to walk around the entire lymphoma section and past the elevators to the children's wing.

At first I was leery of going anywhere near the children. I didn't think my heart could bear seeing so many kids with cancer. As we walked around the corner into that section, I could see a big room that was decorated in bright colors. It was the play room where all the kids that were well enough to be out of bed could go and play together. As we got closer I could see that there were kids in there working with puzzles and playing games together at one of the tables. The room had just about anything a kid would want to play with.

53

God is in the Details

The kids were there with their smaller versions of the chemo pole, and they too had bags of chemicals being infused into their tiny bodies. I almost turned around but George urged me to keep walking. There was one little boy in particular that captured my heart. He was only about three years old, but he was walking with his mother, pushing his own little pole. He had the sweetest little face and the biggest smile that covered his face from ear to ear. It was difficult to walk through there, but we continued on. Nothing had touched my heart quite like seeing those kids. I saw hope in the eyes of their parents as well as fear. I wanted to put my arms around every one of them and tell them that God loved them.

George had several different bags of chemo hanging from his pole. One was Zofran that he was getting for nausea. One was a medication called Mensa that was protecting his kidneys during the chemo, and another one was for allergic reactions. Then there was the chemo itself.

I had discovered what R–Hyper C-VAD stood for by reading a list of all the drugs and putting it together. The R stood for Rituxin; Hyper means more than normal, or excessive amount; C was for the drug Cyclophosphamide; V was for the drug Vincristine; A was for Adriamycin (also called Doxorubicin); and the D was for Dexamethasone. These were the drugs for Cycle A and would be given in rounds 1, 3, and 5.

Along with this list of drugs came the longer list of side effects. I wasn't sure that I wanted to read all of them, but I knew I had to. I needed to stay informed just in case there was ever a problem. Side effects could happen even after George left the hospital and that was the reason that Dr H had wanted us as close to the hospital as possible.

We ate our lunch together and then George decided to take a nap. I headed back to the apartment to get some housework done and to check on the dogs.

The first thing I did was let the dogs out and check on Annie. She seemed anxious to go outside with the other dogs so I went out with them. I started picking up some twigs in the backyard and before I knew it I was dragging branches out front to the curb. It was hot and I was dripping with sweat, but the physical labor was therapeutic. The dogs were enjoying my company and I noticed that even Annie seemed to be enjoying it. She even decided to bark at the neighbor's dogs a few times. I knew I was grasping at straws, but I clung to any sign that maybe she wasn't really as sick as I thought.

Next I went into the kitchen to unload the dishwasher. I noticed water standing in the bottom and realized that it hadn't drained out. I had a dishwasher full of water that I had to dip out with a cup and then I washed the dishes by hand in the sink. I called and left a message with the landlord telling him there was a problem. The dishwasher was brand new and I couldn't imagine why it wouldn't drain!

When I had the kitchen in order I decided to do a load of laundry. I started the washer and when I went back later to take the clothes out, I discovered that the water was still only trickling into the tub. *What next?* "Lord, you are really putting this patience thing to the test!" I called the store where I had rented the washer and dryer and they said they wouldn't be able to come out to fix it until Monday. This was Friday. Now I had a dishwasher that wouldn't drain, a washer full of wet clothes, and it was 97 degrees. All I could think of was a washer full of sour smelling clothes because the washer was in the garage! This was Texas after all, and I was beginning to get a taste of the heat and humidity of August.

I called George to tell him that my visit to see him was going to have to wait until later. I had to do something about the wet clothes, and honestly, I needed to rest.

God is in the Details

Everything was going well at the hospital so I wasn't in a big rush to get there.

Around 6:00 p.m. the doorbell rang. When I opened the door there stood a man who told me he was there to fix my washer! I couldn't believe it. He said he was on his way home and had to pass right by our house so he decided to stop and see if he could help me. *Finally*, someone who actually seemed to care about my situation!

The repair was simple; it took him about five minutes. The water pipe from the house to the washer hoses had been clogged from not being used in a long time. He just cleaned them out and I had a fully operational washing machine! I thanked him for taking his time to stop and asked him how much I owed him. "No charge!" Maybe just maybe my day had turned around and I decided that Texas had some really nice people after all!

I didn't want to go back to the hospital. I needed to get so many things done and now I could actually do some laundry. I made the most of my evening and even managed to pay a few bills and crawl into bed at a reasonable hour for a change.

During the night I faintly remembered hearing some thunder in the distance. I was so tired and for once it was a peaceful sound, but by morning it was a different story. When I woke up the thunder was very loud and when I looked outside, all I could see was the rain pouring out of the downspouts and mud everywhere in the backyard. My first thought was, "Poor Annie," she was terrified of storms.

Once the rain stopped I was able to let the dogs out. The backyard was a disaster. Thick mud was everywhere. I knew it was going to be a real challenge to get the dogs' feet clean when they came inside. Luckily there was a door from the yard into the garage, so I let them all in that way and finally got all twelve feet cleaned off.

Smokey wasn't cooperative at all. She hated getting her

feet washed. She would always try to get away from me and run in the house tracking mud everywhere. She was becoming a huge problem for me. She hadn't made the move to Houston well at all and now she was adding more to my work load than I wanted to handle.

While I was taking a shower, Smokey had gotten sick. When I walked into the kitchen there were piles of diarrhea all over the floor. I couldn't believe that one dog could possibly make all that mess. This wasn't the first time this had happened; it was becoming an almost daily occurrence. As much as I hated to think about it, I knew that something had to be done about it. I didn't have the time or the energy to keep dealing with all of her problems on top of everything else. I made a decision then and there and called the vet.

I had known the day would come, but I hadn't planned for it to be *that* day. I just knew that I had to deal with her before George came home. It was so hard for me because in my own way, I really did love the dog. She had belonged to my dad and I had tried my best to take good care of her after he passed away. I had to do this before my heart got the best of me and I changed my mind.

I cried all the way to the vet's office and a million times I asked my daddy to forgive me for what I was about to do.

When I left the vet's office I went straight to the hospital. I really wanted to spend the whole day with George for a change. I felt like I had been neglecting him, although he didn't feel that way. When I got to the hospital some of their power had been knocked out by the storm. None of the elevators were working and George was on the ninth floor! By the time I made it to his floor, I felt as though I had been mountain climbing. *There are a whole lot of stairs when you climb nine flights of them!*

When I walked into his room, there he sat in his bed with no chemo hooked up to him. I was a bit surprised

God is in the Details

and then a cold dread came over me. I immediately asked, "What's going on, why have they stopped your chemo?" George explained that he had been having some discomfort in his shoulders but he hadn't thought much of it until he went for his walk that morning. Before he got back to his room he had broken out in a cold sweat and wasn't sure he would make it back. He called the nurse and they immediately stopped the chemo and called the doctor. They were waiting for a cardiologist to come in.

We didn't have to wait long before he walked through the door. He was reading George's chart and when he looked up he said, "We have a fly in the ointment!" This was going to delay chemo until they could run some tests to see if there was a problem with George's heart. He would have to stay in the hospital so that meant he would be in longer than the five days we had expected.

Neither of us knew what to say or what to expect from there. All we knew was that they were going to transfer George to the cardiac unit that evening.

I left after that and stopped on the way home to pick up some take-out for my dinner. I knew that Annie would love to have some chicken strips so I ordered some for her as well. She hadn't been eating well at all, but I knew she would eat the chicken if nothing else.

As soon as I opened the door I could tell that she was having problems breathing. She had been sneezing blood for a while but there was more than usual on the floor around her bed. She was losing weight so I was anxious to tempt her with the chicken I had brought. I sat next to her on the floor and fed her little bites from my hand. She ate and I cried. Everything lately was a reminder of just how precious life is and how it can end in an instant. I sat there and cried for Annie and then I cried for George.

Morning came. Annie had had a bad night and I was up with her several times. She was having difficulty breathing

58

and it caused her to have panic attacks. The only thing that helped her was for me to hold her and stroke her head. I knew the time was getting closer when I would have to say good-bye to my baby, but for now I was praying that she would be OK until we knew more about what was going on with George.

When I got to the hospital he tried to look happy to see me, but I could tell that his spirits were really low. This was the first time I had seen him when I felt that he was really discouraged. He always had such a positive attitude and refused to let much get him down. This delay was really hard on him.

They had transferred him to the seventh floor, which was a section in the older part of the hospital. The room he was in now was a far cry from the one he had on the ninth floor. This room was small and very crowded and the only window he had was almost behind his bed. It was dark in there and very depressing. I was only able to stay long enough to see how things were going before I had to leave for a catheter care class that was being given in another part of the hospital. I was required to go to two classes to learn to care for the CVC that was in George's chest. There was special care that needed to be done to it on a daily basis and they wouldn't release him from the hospital until I had passed the class. Today was my first class and I couldn't miss it.

When I got back to his room, I got the news that they would be sending him across the street the following day to St. Luke's Hospital. The Texas Heart Institute is part of St. Luke's and from what he had heard, was one of the best heart centers in the US. He was going to have to be taken by ambulance. *"But the hospital was only across the street!"* I couldn't understand the reason for the ambulance so I asked the nurse when she came in. She said that he had to stay hooked up to the monitors; even though he was only going a short distance he couldn't go without

God is in the Details

the ambulance. With all the precautions they had started taking, my stress level doubled. It made me wonder if they expected him to have a heart attack.

The cardiologist tried to reassure us both by saying that in all likelihood they would probably have to put in a stent and then he would be able to resume the chemo. I tried my best to believe that, *but the alarm bells were going off in my head.*

I left soon after that and when I got to the parking garage I had lost my car! I felt so stupid and panicked at the same time. I had absolutely NO idea on what level I had parked my car. This was a huge multi-level parking garage and for all I knew my car could have been anywhere. My mind just wasn't working very well; I was on overload. I was thankful for the *"panic"* button on my keychain. (Now I know why it's called a panic button). I walked around pushing that red button until I heard my horn honking on the level above. I was so relieved when I finally got to my car. I couldn't wait to get home. It was so hot and humid and I was beyond exhausted. I started the car and dug around in my purse for my prepaid parking ticket. I couldn't get out of the garage without it. I searched my entire purse; I opened the car and got out and looked in the back seat, under the seat, behind the visor, and everywhere I could think to look. *No parking ticket!* My only option was to go to the transportation office and buy a new one.

I had to walk across the entire parking garage, take the elevator to the ground floor, and then walk around the outside of the garage to the opposite end before I got to the office. Once I had my new ticket in my hand, I had to reverse my steps until I was once again at my car. If I thought I was exhausted before, I had no idea *what* I was now. It had been one of those days!

When I got home I had chicken strips for the dogs to share that night. Poor Buddy was feeling a bit ignored, so tonight they both had something to look forward to. They met me at the door with their tails wagging and eyed the bag with interest. They were as happy to see me as I was to see them. They gave me something to look forward to at night when I got home. I even missed Smokey. Thinking about her made me sad, but then, everything these days made me sad.

The next morning I met George at St. Luke's. They had just brought him by ambulance from MDA and I was there waiting when he arrived. They were going to do a heart catheterization to find out if there were any blockages in his heart. All I had been thinking about all night was, "What if this is serious and he can't finish his chemo?" That thought hadn't even entered my mind until I tried to go to sleep. We would find out soon enough. They took him to a room to get him ready to go to surgery and I followed behind, praying that God would calm my nerves.

I spent what seemed like an eternity waiting for the procedure to be over. I was praying that this was just going to be a simple "fix" that wouldn't interfere with chemo. Deep inside, I could feel that knot of fear tightening once more and I knew that I was wishing for a lot. *Nothing had been simple for a very long time.*

I was in a large waiting area, surrounded by people who were waiting just like me. I could overhear conversations, people expressing some of the same fears as mine. It seemed as though everyone had a story to tell, and the more I listened, the more I was struck by the seriousness of some of the conditions that were being treated at that very moment. I had no idea that The Texas Heart Institute was one of the leading hospitals for doing heart transplants. I tried not to think past the procedure that George was undergoing, but now I began to wonder what I was about to hear at any moment. I knew the doctor would be walking through the door very soon and he would tell me what we were facing.

God is in the Details

I was grateful that this heart problem had been discovered before George had a serious heart attack, but now I found myself dreading the news. George had never looked sick! "How could he have had so many things wrong with him and we never knew it?" First it was cancer, and now we could be facing something else that was equally life threatening. Time seemed to stand still and I found myself staring at the door that I knew the doctor would be coming through any time now.

When the doctor came out to talk to me, I could see in his face that things weren't going to be simple, just as I feared. George had two arteries that had 100 percent blockage and a third with about 70 percent. This meant only one thing, *a triple bypass.*

He was in recovery until around 7:00 p.m. The nurse had given him a Neupogen shot for his white blood cells and told us that he would have one each day for five days. His counts had to be normal before his surgery. He had had just enough chemo to cause his counts to drop. This meant the end of chemo for now. It was only temporary, but it was a major setback for George.

The highlight of our day was when George walked in the house and the dogs saw him. I wasn't sure who was the most excited, George or Annie! For a moment I could almost forget that either of them was sick. All I could do was smile and enjoy the moment. It was so good to have him home.

The backyard was fast becoming a serious problem. The dogs weren't able to go out very often because of the mud. They would come in with mud between their toes and all the way up their legs. You can imagine what a job it was getting it out of Annie's long hair. Poor Buddy (he's on the short side); mud would be all the way up to his little belly. I had buckets of water ready in the garage every time I would let them in. We had a routine; they came in and waited very patiently next to the bucket of water until I had them washed, rinsed, and dried. After repeating the "drill" over and over, they both knew it by heart.

Our landlord had called to ask if a deck out back would help with the mud situation. *Would it help?* (I think he was getting tired of hearing me complain.) All of the floors in the house were either white ceramic or ivory colored carpet. I felt as though I had a mop with me the whole time I was at home, mopping up dog tracks. No matter how well I washed their feet, I couldn't get away from that mop. I kept the bedroom doors closed during the day so I could protect the carpet, but cleaning the tile floors was a constant job. Maybe, just maybe, it would stop raining and they would come *tomorrow* and build that deck.

The days all seemed to blend together that week. I had to take George to the hospital once a day for his shot and other than that we didn't do much. I cooked and did house work and George sat in his recliner in front of the TV. He was withdrawn and a little grouchy. My nerves were a bit frayed as well and I found that everything irritated me. I got annoyed at the things George would do and I knew he felt the same about me. We were trying to prepare ourselves for his surgery, but we weren't doing so well. He would forget things and ask me the same question a dozen times and then turn around and ask me again. I could tell that this waiting was getting to him. He had been so strange since the heart problem. I didn't know if it was stress or perhaps some of the medications he was taking. All I knew was that he wasn't the same guy he was a week ago. I wished he would talk to me and let me know what was going on in his head, but he still hadn't learned to share his feelings. *Cancer hadn't changed him but I wondered if heart surgery would.*

Our Annie continued to get worse by the day. That was adding to the stress, and surgery was forever on our minds. We had been in Houston less than a month. It was hard to believe all that we had gone through, and *we had only just begun.*

God is in the Details

Sleep was a problem. Our neighbors were three medical students who were either gone and leaving their dogs outdoors to bark all night, or having loud parties outside our bedroom window. Those two big dogs barked non-stop day and night and no amount of complaining seemed to make a difference. I called the landlord to complain. I had discovered that he was *their* landlord as well so I expected something to be done about it. I was beginning to question whether this was really where we were supposed to live or not. I was so sure that God had given us this house, but I was beginning to think it may be temporary and that we had needed it just to get us to Houston.

I still had not heard another word about a deck and it was raining again! The mud was so bad that I actually lost a sandal when I stepped out the back door. All I did these days was wash dogs' feet and try to keep George in a decent mood. His attitude was getting worse and I was trying my best not to take it personally, but it was almost impossible at times. I felt that the harder I tried to help him, the more impatient he got with me. I couldn't wait until a surgery date was scheduled; I think the waiting was getting to both of us.

The call finally came and surgery was scheduled for Tuesday. That was only four days away. All of a sudden I didn't want to be alone while George was in surgery.

I called our daughter Cathy and asked her if she would come to Houston for a week. She wasn't working and was happy to be able to help me. We made reservations for her to arrive on Monday. I had something positive to look forward to and my mood changed dramatically. I hadn't realized just how much I had been dreading being alone.

Saturday was our last trip to the hospital so we stopped at Starbuck's before coming home. It was one of our last outings before the big day. When we got home, the sky looked threatening and by two we were having a major storm. Annie was miserable. She was so frightened of the

64

loud thunder and finally just decided to climb into George's lap. Before long, his lap was full; Buddy decided to join Annie. I was thinking about how many times I was going to have to wash muddy paws until the mud dried up.

On Sunday we decided that we needed to get out of the house. I had done laundry all day the day before and had tried to stay ahead of the mud. A movie sounded good so we decided to go see *Manchurian Candidate*. It was a good movie, but hard to follow at first. I think it did George a lot of good to get away and get his mind on something besides chemo and surgery. He actually perked up and wasn't nearly as ornery as he had been all week. It was a good thing that we had such a pleasant day; I couldn't say as much for our night.

Annie woke me up in the night; she was having a very hard time breathing. I got up and got her some water and that seemed to help a little. All of her breathing seemed to be through her mouth now and when she slept she got very dry. She still didn't seem to be in pain and I was grateful for that at least. She had eaten a little the night before and I had given her a chew bone. It was wonderful to see her enjoy that bone. She still had that sparkle in her eyes when she saw me take her bone out of the cabinet. *She loves those chew bones.* I sat up with her until she had calmed down and then we both went back to bed. The panic attacks always seemed to be at night when she was trying to sleep. She would get frantic when she couldn't breathe. I knew the time was coming, but I tried not to think about it. I wanted things to settle down just long enough to get George through surgery.

We received so many e-mails from home as well as tons of cards and notes from people at church telling us that they were praying for us. *I knew they were,* because I could feel the strength of those prayers. I don't think I could have gone through everything thus far without the *absolute*

God is in the Details

certainty that God loved us and that He was walking our journey with us. Sometimes we lose track of what is really important. Not too long ago my life seemed to be going along smoothly. I was busy complaining about this and that and too busy to really appreciate all that I had. Life had made a huge turnaround in those past few months, and in a lot of ways, nothing would ever be the same. My prayer was that I wouldn't soon forget all that God was doing in my life. He was teaching me important things and I knew that He *expected me to be more than I was today.* I felt that I was taking some giants steps in my faith.

I met a lot of great people online who were dealing with MCL, either as a patient or a caregiver. I decided to start a website where we could all go to share our experiences. I was looking for a support group online and I found a terrific group of people who understood my fear. The group had been a tremendous help to me and I hoped that I had been able to support all of them as well. Two of them were coming to MD Anderson for tests and I was hoping that we would be able to meet. I felt as though we had become a family. I knew that if anyone could understand what I was feeling, it was them.

Monday was surprisingly a decent day, considering that the next day would be THE DAY. We left early for the airport. So far I hadn't ventured out on the expressways in Houston very often, but to get to the airport, I had no choice. George wanted to stop at a surplus store on the way and putter around to see what all they had. We stopped for ice cream and then got back on the road. The whole drive made me so nervous that even the soles of my feet were sweating. I had never driven on any highway that compared to those in Houston. I think everyone has a bad case of road rage. The road signs are all confusing and the exit ramps are "just wrong." Besides, whoever heard of an HOV lane? Certainly not me! I have no idea what that is! I'm not sure what the biggest stressor for me was, the amount of traffic or the speed at which everyone drives!

Cathy's plane was twenty minutes late and they had left one of her suitcases in Detroit. *Why was I surprised?* I should be used to everything being difficult by now. Regardless, she was in Houston and I was so happy to see her I could hardly contain myself. *Finally* I had someone to talk to and someone to be by my side for a whole week.

We went out for dinner and once we got home all the kids called to wish their dad good luck the next day. We also got a HUGE surprise. Our pastor from our church in Michigan called to say he had just arrived in Houston and would be at the hospital the next day. Surprise was an understatement! I was speechless if that was possible. We had no idea that he was planning to be there and that's how he had planned it. He was going to just show up at the hospital the next day, but he decided he needed to call to see what time surgery was scheduled. The hospital wouldn't give out that information.

What a privilege it is to belong to a church like ours. Our church family was so faithful in their prayers and never forgot our needs while we were away. (And now our pastor was here!) God really knows our needs before we even know them ourselves. He had put the desire in our pastor's heart to be with us and that was *exactly* what we needed.

George and I went to bed fairly early. It was going to be a very early morning and an even longer day. Before he went to sleep George wanted to tell me something. He said, "In case something should happen tomorrow and surgery doesn't go well, I just want you to know that I love you very much and appreciate everything you do for me." When he said that, I knew that he was more than a little anxious about the outcome.

Five

·· ✿ ··

Surgery day, August 31, had arrived. Cathy, George, and I got to the hospital at 5:30 a.m. and found out that George was second on the schedule. "Now why did we have to be there *before* daylight if he wasn't going to surgery for a few hours?" All we were told was that all surgery patients had to report at that time. This did not set well with me, but again, what choice did we have?

Pastor John arrived around 6:15, just about the time they sent us to the "holding room" as I called it. It was just another waiting room full of outdated magazines and sleepy people waiting to hear their name called. We were happy to see John when he came in. He has such a presence about him that he can calm a whole room of people. (I guess that's why he is a pastor!) I was really happy to have him and Cathy with us that morning. The hour may have been early, but the company was fantastic.

John and George had quite a conversation going, as did Cathy and I. It helped to pass the time. Around

10:15 someone finally came to take us downstairs to the *real* waiting room. This time Cathy and John went into that room and I went with George to the pre-op area. I couldn't believe that we had been at the hospital for five hours already and this was as far as we had gotten. It was another forty-five minutes before George was actually taken to surgery.

I kissed him just as they were about to wheel him through the door. I felt my heart would break as I watched him joking with the nurses and the guys taking him to surgery. "How like him to be able to find humor in any circumstance!" However, the feeling that this could be the last time I would ever see him dampened the humor for me.

I found my way back out to the waiting room where Cathy and John were, and we headed to the cafeteria to eat lunch. It seemed like we had been there for days already and surgery was just beginning. It had been hours since either of us had eaten. We ate lunch and talked and waited...and drank a lot of coffee. We talked and waited; we waited and talked. The wait seemed endless.

A surgery tech came out about every hour and a half to give us a report. This gave us something to look forward to as well as relieve a little stress. She was very good about making sure we knew exactly what was happening in the O.R. The 12:30 report was that finding good leg veins to use had been difficult. The chest wasn't opened yet but that was next on the schedule. I ran to the phone to report to all the kids back home, and we resumed our vigil.

The next report came a little after 1:30; the chest was open and the actual bypass had begun. So far all was going well so I decided this would be a good time to go home to let the dogs out and feed them. I felt anxious about leaving, but I knew I had someone there to call me if I was needed. I made the trip home and back in record time and was back in time for the 3:00 report.

God is in the Details

Everything was going well at that point and the tech said, *"normal and routine."* She thought that by the 4:30 report she would be able to tell us that the surgery was all but over and that they were closing the chest.

I know we talked all day, but I honestly don't remember much that was said. It seemed like a jumble of words here and there; I had so many thoughts running through my head. Pastor John was such a blessing to me. He was there giving his support and I know that he had been talking to God all day. (If your pastor can't reach God, you need to find a new one!) I had no doubt that those prayers were being answered as we waited.

The report at 4:30 was just what we had hoped for. They were getting ready to close the chest and this should take about forty-five minutes and the surgeon would come out to talk to me. Our wait was almost over.

Almost to the minute, out comes this young surgeon fresh from O.R., still in scrubs and a very sweaty hat. I had actually never met the surgeon before that very minute. *I was a bit taken aback when I saw how young he was.* He looked like a mere boy to me. Once he began to talk, I realized that he was very capable and that put my mind at ease. He explained the whole process to us. He said that he had thought he would be doing a triple bypass but once he was inside, he realized that there was a lot more work to be done.

He ended up doing a quadruple bypass and also did what he called an endarterectomy, a procedure to clean out a fifth artery that was too small to actually bypass. He compared that procedure to a carotid surgery where they clean out the arteries in a person's neck. He said that they had worked very hard during this surgery because George's arteries were such a mess. He also told us that George was a very lucky man to have had the surgery before he had a serious heart attack. There was no evidence that he could see to indicate any previous heart attacks and no damage to his heart muscle. He classified George as a walking time bomb ready to go off and could see no reason why he hadn't suffered a very serious heart attack already. He went on to say that he had done many bypass surgeries where people had suffered multiple heart attacks prior to their surgery but few of them had blockages as bad as George had.

In the coming days, George was telling people, *"God allowed me to have cancer so I could get my heart fixed."* I can't say that I disagree with that statement. I was to find out much later that he had been having symptoms for a long time and had never said one word to me or to anyone else. He had just gone on with his life, completely ignoring it. I'm sure he would have done the exact same thing with lymphoma if I had given him a chance.

Before the surgeon left us, I needed to ask him something for George. George has a tattoo on his chest of an eagle that he had gotten while he was in the Marines. He had told the doctor before surgery to make sure he lined up that eagle before he sewed him back up. The doctor laughed and told me he thought he had done a good job on the eagle and that George should be very pleased. It was good to be a little lighthearted before I had to walk into the critical care unit for the first time.

At 6 p.m. the critical care nurse came out to say that two of us could go back to the unit to see George for ten minutes. Cathy opted not to go in so that John could go in with me. I was so thankful to have a big strong man with me when I went in for the first time.

We went in together but had to stop to wash our hands before we could enter the area where George was. I had tried all day to prepare myself for what I was about to see, but one step into that area and I knew that there was no preparation in the world that could have gotten me ready for that scene. My shaking started as soon as the doctor left, and I found that it got a lot worse once I stepped into that room.

God is in the Details

The first thing I saw was George lying there in bed hooked up to a ventilator. I had known ahead of time that he would be on the ventilator, but I could hardly bear to look at him. I had no idea he would have so many tubes everywhere. He had two tubes in his chest that looked like garden hoses. (That is no exaggeration!) He had another tube in his mouth and down his throat that was removing his stomach fluids, he had oxygen, a rather large IV in the artery in the right side of his neck, IVs in his hands, a catheter in his bladder, a drain in his thigh, as well as wires sticking out of his chest. Those wires were there in case he needed an external pacemaker at any time. *There wasn't a place on his body that wasn't connected to something.*

I was standing very close to John this whole time because I wasn't sure whether I would remain standing or if I was going to faint. Two nurses were sitting with him, one on either side of the bed, watching monitors and taking notes. *The sound of the ventilator breathing for George seemed to fill the entire room.* I felt sick as I stood there watching everything that was going on, but at the same time it was reassuring to know that they were taking such excellent care of him.

I walked up to the side of his bed so that I could touch him and tell him that I was there. His arm was so cold and he was totally unresponsive. (If he were to wake up he could become agitated and try to pull the tube out of his throat.) They would keep him this way for several more hours and then they would gradually wake him up. At that time they would test his breathing and if he could breathe on his own they would take him off the ventilator. I knew that was going to be the hard part for him and I was glad that I wouldn't have to see it when it happened.

The nurse asked us to leave then, so I bent down to kiss him good-bye. I was remembering the last time I had kissed him. *"Had it only been just hours before?"* The day seemed endless. I had been so afraid that I would never see him again when they had taken him to surgery, yet here we were. He was still with me and now I could only pray that he was going to be OK. No words could ever describe my feelings at that moment. *Thank you, God.*

John and I found Cathy in the waiting area. The minute she saw us she stood up and rushed over to me to ask about her dad. I knew that my face showed all the stress I had been under and I had tears running down my face...*happy tears.* All I could do was hug her and assure her that dad was going to be OK.

We dropped John off at his hotel with plans to meet the next morning around 10 a.m. He would go with us to see George before he left for the airport. I hope I thanked him for being with us that day. I can't say for sure that I did because some of that day was a blur to me. I would never be able to express in words what his gesture meant to all of us no matter how hard I tried.

Cathy and I went back to see George that night at the 8:30 visiting hour. She hadn't seen her dad since before he went to surgery and wanted to see him before we went to bed. This time when we went in his room, he was trying to wake up and was gagging on the ventilator tube and trying to pull it out. It wasn't a pleasant sight for either of us. When I would try to talk to him, he would become more agitated. They gave him some morphine to keep him quiet, and Cathy and I decided we needed to leave and let the medication work.

I called the hospital around 11 p.m. to check on him. They were just getting ready to take him off the ventilator. I was actually able to relax then, just knowing that he would be rid of a least one of the many tubes. By 3 a.m. I was on the phone again. This time when the nurse answered, she asked me if I wanted to talk to him! OH MY GOSH...I didn't know what to say. I had no idea he would be able to talk to me. He sounded very medicated and very hoarse, but

God is in the Details

he could *talk* and it was only fifteen hours post surgery. I was so happy. I told God over and over how grateful I was and I thanked Him for all that He had brought us through.

They moved George from critical care at 3 p.m. the day after surgery. He was so medicated that he had no idea where he was or what was going on. He had no idea what he had just gone through and I saw that as a blessing. They told me he was doing extremely well, so I had to take their word for it. He looked awful to me. I had expected him to be a little "out of it," but I didn't expect this.

When Cathy and I got to the room where they would be bringing him, I took one look around and knew this wasn't going to work. The room was so small and crowded that there wasn't even room for a nurse to get to both sides of the bed. One side of the bed was shoved up next to a wall and the other side had a space of about three feet between it and the other bed that was in the room. It was so hot and stuffy and there was no place for Cathy or me to sit. I started complaining as soon as the nurse came in. She told me that this was the only room available and that this was where he was going to be. She didn't know me very well! I asked her to find a supervisor for me, but in the meantime George had just been brought to the room.

I couldn't even get near him. I wanted to talk to him and hold his hand, but there was no way. By the time they had him and all the monitors in that tiny space there was no room for anything else. The longer I waited to speak to a supervisor the more upset I got.

I didn't have to wait all that long, but it seemed like a long time to me. When she came into the room I told her that this wasn't acceptable and that I wanted him in another room immediately. She was sweet and accommodating and told me she would see what she could do. When she came back in she had a private room waiting for him!

She was an angel is disguise. I remembered something

I had written down in one of my many notebooks; it said, *"Angels come to help and guide us in as many guises as there are people who need their assistance. Sometimes we see their ethereal heavenly shadow, bright with light and radiance. Sometimes we only feel their nearness or hear their whisper, and sometimes they look no different from ourselves."* (Eileen Elias Freeman)

Once he was in his "new" room, Cathy and I were able to be comfortable as well. The room was large and much cooler and I was glad that I had pushed the issue. George needed all the comfort he could have and I made it my job to see that he got it. His pain had grown pretty intense and some of it was from being moved around so much. He didn't know enough to ask for pain medication, so I asked the nurse to give him a shot of Demerol. She wanted to give him a pain pill! That wasn't going to happen if I had anything to say about it. I knew the doctor had ordered something stronger than a *pill* so I asked her to go and check his chart. It was barely twenty-four hours since his surgery and I was determined that he was going to be as pain free as possible. They gave him pain *"shots"* for the next two days!

The medication kept him pretty "looped" and out of it most of the time. He would tell Cathy and me about all the things he saw during the night. He had all sorts of imaginary "friends" that visited him in the wee hours. Every morning he told us a different story about things that had gone on in his room. We laughed at him because he reminded us both of my dad when he had taken some medications that made him hallucinate. We decided that it was safe to laugh at him because he wasn't going to remember it anyway.

The one thing that George *did* remember was a nurse trying to put compression stockings on him after surgery. The leg they had taken his veins out of for the bypass was extremely painful. (He talked about those stockings for

God is in the Details

weeks afterward.) In his opinion that was the worst pain he had ever felt. What amazed me was the fact that he was in critical care when they put those stockings on and he remembered it, even though he had no recollection of anything else that had happened to him. It must have been extreme for him to feel it through all the morphine he was on. (Even after he came home, he continued to complain every time I had to put those stockings on.)

Each day was getting better than the day before. George was now able to be up and walking once the chest tubes were removed. I was there with him the day they came in to take them out. I stayed in the room with him for most of the things they did to him, but this was one time the nurse asked me to leave the room. When I went back in, I could tell that it *had not* been a pleasant experience for him. He told me that it had been very painful but he felt a lot better knowing that those tubes were gone for good. I didn't even let myself try to imagine how those tubes had to come out of his chest. That was more information than I needed.

Next came the wires that had been sticking out of his chest. He wasn't happy with that little experience either, but each time a tube or wire was removed, he was that much closer to being able to go home. He continued to improve and the nurses and doctors all said it was due to his positive attitude. I think he felt that if he had made it this far, then he was up for whatever was ahead.

Cathy had to leave on Saturday and I became instantly depressed again. It was just so wonderful to have her there. We were able to enjoy our time together even under the circumstances. We had even managed to get out to lunch a couple of times and to do a little shopping. There were times when George was busy with physical therapy so we had some free time of our own. I was going to miss her company and most of all having her support. I had started to get used to being alone, but having her there had spoiled me.

Diane Pretty

Sunday at 3:00 I brought George home from the hospital. He came home on the sixth day after surgery, and everyone at the hospital said that was remarkable for all he had gone through. He was happy to be out of the hospital and I was equally happy to have him home with me. Our little family was complete. Annie was still with us but I knew that she was getting worse every day. For now, I was content just to have us all together.

E-mails continued to come every day with wishes for a speedy recovery. Prayers continued for both of us and all that was still ahead. It helped me to know that we had all that support from friends and family. For most people who had just undergone a heart bypass, this was the end of hospitals and the healing was all that was left. Not so for George; he still had six treatments of chemotherapy ahead. Once he was able to start the treatments again, he would have to start all over. The two days that he had already finished didn't count. He would start at square one.

More rain had come. I was about over the edge for sure by now with the situation in the backyard. One day I finally decided to look for another house to rent. I had been looking around in the neighborhood and had found one on the next street. We could have it if we wanted it, but I decided to give our landlord one more chance to make things right. I called to tell him that we would be moving if he didn't do something about that deck he had promised us. I really didn't want to even think about all the work a move would entail, but I knew that something had to be done, and *soon*.

The neighbors had been partying nonstop as well and that was getting on my nerves. I had explained it all to the landlord many times and the noise would stop for a little while, but then it was back to *"Party Central."* I had begun to realize why he didn't push the issue with the guys next door; they were long-term tenants and we were only staying for a few months. I guess I could understand that,

God is in the Details

but at the same time, I didn't feel it was right for anyone to be able to disturb their neighbors to the extent they were.

I knew for a fact that if George didn't get his rest, his healing wouldn't go as well.

A short time later the landlord called me back to say he was going to have a crew there the next day to clean up some of the yard and that he would be having the deck built. He told me that he sympathized with our situation and hated to see us pack up and move since George was so recently out of surgery. This was his last chance and if nothing came of it, I would definitely be looking for another place to live. Miraculously, all was quiet for the next couple of weeks. No parties, no barking dogs...*What a relief.*

The first week home, George did exceptionally well. He was starting to get out every morning to walk. The first morning he walked to the corner and felt very proud of himself. The next day he ventured around the block and was surprised at how good he felt. In no time at all, we were both walking a mile every morning. I hated to admit it, but he could out-walk me. He was amazed at the energy he felt since he was getting so much circulation through his body. I would tease him and say, "Hey, you have a totally rebuilt engine and I'm still running on my original!" We were enjoying this time together and didn't even mind that the temperature was already in the nineties by seven each morning. *Gotta love Houston in September.*

The deck was finally finished and the yard was cleaned up, so we ventured out to Lowe's to look for a small barbeque grill. The deck wasn't "great" but it served the purpose and I was anxious to get a couple of outside chairs so that we could sit out there when the weather permitted. We had fun shopping and when we got home, I made our first dinner on our new grill. *I was happy.* I was *really* happy for the first time in a very long time. George was improving all the time and he had such a healthy glow to

Diane Pretty

his complexion. I was beginning to get used to the peace that we were enjoying. I loved sitting out on the deck every morning, drinking my coffee with the two dogs at my feet. Yes, life was good for a brief moment in time.

A week after George came home, he had an appointment for a follow-up to have his stitches removed. He received an excellent report from the doctor and was released to do pretty much anything he wanted to do, with the exception of lifting anything heavier than twenty-five pounds. The surgeon told us it would take a little while for the chest bones to completely grow back together, but not to worry, they were permanently wired together inside his chest! (I wondered if that meant he would set off the alarm at the airport!) He just needed to take it easy for awhile, but eventually he would be taken off the lifting restrictions. Unless anything unforeseen should happen, he would see his oncologist in about five weeks to schedule his chemo. I was living in the moment and trying to forget all about chemo. The longer I could avoid that reality, the better.

We were still walking every morning, regardless of the temperature. We really enjoyed seeing how far we could walk, so we started adding a block or two every day. Before we knew it, we were up to two miles. George's goal was to reach three miles, but I was more than content with the two miles that I was walking. I told him that if he wanted to be a "show off" then go for it! (He did.) Before too many more days had passed, he was doing those three miles with no problem at all.

Sunday night, September 30, turned out to be a bad night for Annie. We had gone to bed fairly early that night, only to be awakened by the sound of her pacing the floor. She would lie back down on her bed and try to get comfortable, but then the pacing would start again. She started making a very loud noise that I had never heard before. I jumped out of bed and picked her up right away

God is in the Details

and carried her into the family room. I wasn't sure what was happening to her, but I knew she was struggling to breathe and she was scared. I held her on my lap and she put her head on my shoulder while I stroked her head and talked to her. She got very still and I thought she had died.

George came out of the bedroom to see what was going on. He sat down next to me and put his hand on her back and just looked at me. I was crying and so was he. We were both sure she was dead. We sat there for a while and finally she opened her eyes and just looked at me. I couldn't believe it. I must have calmed her down enough to where she wasn't struggling for breath and she had just gone to sleep. I told George to go back to bed and I would be there in a little while. I sat up with Annie for the longest time, just holding her and crying. My vet had been right, "Annie was telling me that the time had come."

I called the vet's office early the next morning. They said I could bring her in whenever I was ready. (I would never be ready!) I had planned to take her by myself and spare George the trip, but he insisted on going with me. We both cried all the way across town. I could tell by the look in Annie's eyes that she was ready. *We said good-bye to our baby.*

Buddy was waiting for us when we got home. He was lost for days afterward. He had come to Houston with his two friends, and now they were both gone. He moped around and wouldn't eat. He wouldn't go outside unless I went with him. I felt so sorry for him but I didn't know what to do for him…I didn't know what to do for ME.

One night, a couple of days after Annie left us, we found Buddy in our bed waiting for us when we got to the bedroom. I started to make him get down and get on his own bed, but the look in his eyes broke my heart. I looked at George and he looked at me and in silent agreement, we acquired a new bed partner.

80

Six

It was almost time for us to make the oncology appointment, but first we needed to go to the infusion department at the hospital to get George's CVC checked. After we were done there, we went to pick up a new batch of bandages at central supply and then to the pharmacy for a new prescription of Heparin. (I used the Heparin to flush the CVC to prevent clots from forming in the line.) We got that taken care of and had just gotten back to the parking garage when George suddenly stopped. He said, "I think we need to go the ER." I turned to him and asked, "What's wrong? Why do we need to go to ER?" I couldn't imagine why he had said that. I had *no* clue that anything was wrong. *Then* he told me that he had been having sharp twinges in his chest all morning and had never said a thing to me. He had hoped they would stop, but so far they hadn't. I knew this was something that needed to be checked right away so I started looking for a wheelchair. I should have known he would refuse the

God is in the Details

wheelchair, and we had a very long walk back to where the ER was located.

I signed him in at the desk and went to sit next to him. He asked me, "Is it hot in here or is it just me?" Next he started sweating and all I could think of was that he was having a heart attack for sure. I went straight to the desk and told them that I thought my husband was having a heart attack. That got their attention and within two minutes we were through the doors and George was on a stretcher. The triage nurse was asking questions and an intern was taking his blood pressure, heart rate, and temperature. Everything was happening at once. They weren't taking any chances so they took him to a small room and hooked him up to a monitor and started doing an EKG. Blood was drawn and before we knew it a cardiologist was in the room. He examined George and looked over his EKG. He said that everything so far looked OK, but to play it safe, they were going to keep him overnight. He wanted to repeat the EKGs and do blood work every six hours to see if his heart enzymes remained stable.

When he was all settled, the nurse told me to go home and rest because they wanted George to stay quiet and try to sleep before his next EKG. I went home but I called around 10:30 to check on him. The nurse said he was still awake and had the call transferred into his room. I asked him how he was feeling and his reply was, "I'd feel a lot better if I could get comfortable on this hard bed!" He told me that the ER was exceptionally busy and that made it exceptionally loud. He said his pillow was too flat and his blanket was too short; I knew he was in for a very long night! He was going to ask for a sleeping pill as soon as we hung up. I knew he was *not* going to be happy when I saw him the next morning.

I was up early and back to ER the next morning. Sure enough…*he was not happy.*

They had finally given him a sleeping pill at 1:30 but had to wake him up at 3.00 for his next tests. That made no sense to me at all. He had been awake all night and was groggy from the sleeping pill. The chest pains had stopped but they had one more round of tests to do at 9:00; then they would decide if he could go home or not.

We saw a doctor around 10:00. He explained to us that George's heart seemed perfectly fine but that sometimes during the healing process after bypass surgery, the muscles in the chest can become a little aggravated and actually have spasms. He was pretty sure that's what was happening in George's case. He would be getting the release papers ready and as soon as that was done, George was free to go.

Two hours later we were still waiting. By this time George was becoming a bit irate and when the nurse came in with papers in hand, all he could say was, "It's about time!" Finally he was free to leave!

The chest pains didn't return and we were both relieved. One day as I was sitting in the family room trying to read a book, my mind kept wandering over the last couple of months and all that had happened in our lives. It occurred to me that if it hadn't been for the heart surgery, George would have already completed his *third* round of chemo and he would be at the halfway mark. I knew that God had his purpose for all of it and even though it didn't coincide with our timing, we had finally accepted the delay. Now we were even beginning to look forward to the chemo again, because that would bring us closer to the time when we could go home.

I had kept myself busy during the past few weeks trying new recipes and putting together jigsaw puzzles. George had really enjoyed all the new dishes that I had prepared and I had to admit, I was really pleased with the way they were turning out. Both of us were getting quite good at puzzles as well. I couldn't remember a time when we had

God is in the Details

spent so much time together and had really enjoyed some of the very simplest things in life. Some days we sat on the deck and talked and enjoyed watching Buddy play with the dogs next door through the fence. Our days were slow and lazy with no interruptions, and I was at peace.

This was the first time since we had moved to Houston that the pace had slowed down enough so that I could rest. We had needed this time together and I could see that we were growing closer than we had been in a long time. George still didn't like to share his feelings with me but I was getting pretty good at "reading" him. No matter what we had to face, we would face it together. I was sure all those prayers that were being said on our behalf had a lot to do with this closeness that we had. *God's timing is always perfect, no matter what!*

October 14. The day of the oncology appointment had arrived. We were more than ready by now, or at least I thought we were. Dr H told us that he was going to admit George to the hospital that same day. I certainly wasn't expecting to hear that. Things never went as planned, but over the past two months we had learned to "expect the unexpected."

We went home and I packed a bag for George to take with him to the hospital and then we waited for the call to come saying they had a bed ready. Admissions at MDA weren't like admissions at other hospitals. Beds were always on demand for chemo patients and when chemo was finished for one patient, the room was cleaned and the next patient was admitted. It didn't matter if it was midnight when the call came; we went whenever they said "ready."

We got to the hospital around 6 p.m. I knew there would be the usual wait and I was correct. Chemo began at 11:30 that night. This time they told us that the Rituxin shouldn't cause the same side effects as it did the first time. After that first infusion, patients seemed to have a much easier time with it. Boy, I wish we had known that before; it would have taken a little bit of the dread out of starting chemo again.

The next morning everything was going great. The night had gone smoothly and there had been no side effects at all. I was concerned about how chemo was affecting his heart more than anything. After all he had gone through to get to this point, I didn't want anything to damage his "new" heart. I voiced my concerns to Dr H and he said, "George's heart is in much better condition to tolerate the chemo than it was before." All I had to do now was convince myself that we were doing the best possible thing for George and leave the rest in God's very capable hands.

Day two went well as did day three. One problem that George was having was his diabetes. One of the drugs in Cycle A was a steroid and that really caused his glucose to go sky high. They had started him on insulin right away, but his counts were still over the roof. He had also started retaining fluids, but we were told that was to be expected. His feet and legs were so swollen that he could hardly get his slippers on; in fact, sometimes he couldn't! The leg where they had taken the veins from for his bypass was the worst.

They encouraged him to walk as much as possible, but they didn't have to do much persuading. George had continued to walk three miles every day and by the time chemo had started again, he was in great shape. In fact, he was out walking the halls every morning before breakfast. Everyone on his floor recognized him because he was out there talking to people he met, always with some words of encouragement to the other patients. (The fact that he wore his military camouflage hat didn't hurt!) A few of the nurses would tease him and ask if he was trying out for the Olympics.

It just so happened that one of the guys I had met online through my website was at MDA having his first round

God is in the Details

of chemo as well. Imagine our surprise when I saw his name on the door just down the hall from George! His name is Norm and he and his wife live near Abilene, Texas. We tapped on his door and went in to introduce ourselves. Norm was a day ahead of George in the "chemo department" and they had a lot of notes to compare. I was glad they were getting their chemo at the same time because it gave them both someone to visit with and talk to during the long hours at the hospital. I felt as though I already knew Norm because we had shared a lot of e-mails in the prior weeks.

The wife of another man on our website was coming to the hospital to meet us; they lived in Houston. Her husband, Charles, had already gone through the chemo a few months ago and was doing really well. Bridget and I had written back and forth and she had helped me so much to deal with all the fears that I had about the chemo. She had offered an ear when I needed to talk and a shoulder whenever I needed one. She was encouraging to me and was always optimistic about the recovery. I was blessed to have met her and I appreciated her support so much.

God was sending so many people into our lives who were both loving and encouraging. Many of the nurses would stop in his room and share their faith with us. I had never been in a hospital where people were so ready to talk about God. We never saw a single person come into the room who wasn't happy and smiling and ready to lift our spirits. Some may say it was part of their "training" but I knew better. These people had a genuine love for God and they saw their job as a ministry. They always went out of their way to make sure that we were both as comfortable as possible and had everything we needed. I began to feel as though these strangers were the family that I didn't have there in Houston. Whenever I left the hospital at night, I always felt at peace knowing that my husband was in good hands.

Diane Pretty

Day five. Things were still going well. Today they were starting Doxorubicin, or Adriamycin as it's also called. The nickname for this drug around the hospital is The Red Devil. It's actually a reddish color and is the one chemo that would be the most damaging to the heart. I prayed, "God, give me strength" as they started the infusion. I was trying very hard to stay calm and not upset George with my concerns, but when I looked at that poison dripping into his body, it made me weak in the knees. I had already noticed the warning label on the bags of chemo. They all said "Do not handle without gloves." That really did nothing to relieve my fear. *The nurses had to have gloves on just to handle those bags of chemo and it was dripping into Georges veins.* I knew that George had read those labels as well and I was sure he had the same concerns, but he was amazingly strong and determined. He kept reminding me that when this bag was finished he could go home.

We had a diabetes education class to attend that afternoon at the hospital. That would help keep our minds off the chemo infusion for awhile. We had to attend the class so that I could learn to give George his insulin injections at home. He was going to need insulin along with his regular medications to control his diabetes while he was undergoing the chemo. We left the room pushing the chemo pole ahead of us...George, me, and The Red Devil.

We got home around noon the next day. George was feeling great and Buddy and I were both happy to have him home with us again. I was hoping that all the treatments would go as well as the first one had. I knew that wasn't likely to happen, but I could hope. He was to begin having Neupogen shots the next day for his white blood cell counts, so that would mean a daily trip to the hospital for ten days. It was going to be a busy three weeks until the next round of chemo. He would have to go to the hospital the next week for a few hours to get an infusion of

God is in the Details

Vincristine, but he wouldn't have to be admitted for that. We had appointments every few days at the lab, and of course the appointment at Fast Track where we would see a nurse and they would go over the labs with us.

I made a stop at the pharmacy after I had George settled at home. I had a handful of prescriptions that he would be taking for the next ten days. There was a prescription for nausea, one for pain, one for sleep, two antibiotics, two antiviral meds, and two for his heart. There was also one for a mouth rinse that he would need to use several times a day for the mouth sores that would be showing up any day now. I couldn't believe that he had to take so much medicine. I just know it would have killed me if I had to take all that. George is tough for sure.

October 22. We started our daily trips to the hospital that day. I had planned to be busy but we had one unexpected stop before we could come home. George was in the ER again. This time it was for some rectal bleeding that had started the night before. They had told us to go to ER if he had any unusual bleeding of any kind. It turned out to be mild and not anything to become alarmed about unless it should get worse or continue. I was relieved and George was complaining about me insisting that he go in to be checked. He hated ER by now and I couldn't blame him, but it was "better to be safe than sorry."

Monday found us at Fast Track. We had already been to the lab for blood work and now had a two-hour wait before we would get the results. I never could understand why they called it *"fast"* anything. Nothing was fast, believe me. Everywhere we went it was wait and wait some more. We had decided in the very beginning that we had to get accustomed to waiting. Everywhere you look there are people who have cancer. We understood that these people were all very ill and that waiting our turn was part of the process. I made sure I always had a book with me. In each waiting area there are plenty of books and magazines as well as jigsaw puzzles spread out on tables for people to work on while they wait. They do everything possible to make the waiting as easy as possible. They even have courtesy carts that come by with free coffee, tea, and cookies or snacks.

When it was our turn, we went in to see the nurse and found out that George's counts were low, which meant he was neutropenic. He wouldn't be out in public for awhile because his immunity was low and there was a chance he could pick up an infection. That meant NO shopping for him. (That was no punishment; he hates shopping.) This called for a little *"duck mask"* to be worn when he was around people. When we left the clinic, George was quacking at everyone he passed.

He seemed so tired this week. I noticed that he wasn't keeping his normal pace when we went walking and that bothered him a lot. We still walked on the days that he felt up to it, but I could see the changes in him since his first round of chemo. I could now begin to imagine what must be in store for him over the next few months. It hurt my heart to see him pushing himself without much success. He was so full of energy after his bypass and I knew it was the hardest on him when he realized those days were gone for awhile. I wished with all my heart that he didn't have to go through any more and that we could just go home!

The first day that George was able to leave the house without his mask, we went to meet our friends Nancy and Rondi for lunch. They were back in Houston again for Rondi's check-up so we decided to get together before they had to leave for home. We had a wonderful time. This was the second time I had seen them since we were in Houston, but this was a first for George. He hadn't seen them for several years and really enjoyed "catching up." We remembered Rondi as a cute little kid with straight

God is in the Details

blonde hair and we were both having a hard time getting used to her "cancer hair." It had come back almost black and curly!! That started a conversation about George's hair and we all had our own opinion as to how we thought he would look *post-chemo*. (I was hoping for bright red curls!) Rondi was all grown up now with two little kids of her own. It was hard to believe how fast time had gone. Neither of us were ready for lunch to end, but they had a plane to catch and I knew that George was getting tired. I thanked Nancy again for taking the time to call me and encourage me to bring George to MD Anderson. (God was preparing our way even then.)

On our way home we talked about all the people that we saw every time we went to the clinic. We rarely ever saw the same person more than a few times, and that made us wonder just how many people in the world had cancer. No one can ever describe how it feels to be surrounded by hundreds of people, all fighting this battle, unless you experience it for yourself. Some days I felt as though I was in constant prayer for the needs of those people. I felt a connection to all of them, whether we spoke or not. Some of them were anxious to talk and would strike up a conversation, while others would go on their way, heads down, just trying to get through the day. (My heart breaks for all of them.) Once in awhile when I would be talking to someone, they would reach out and hug me. I was always ready for those hugs and it made me even more aware of our need for human touch. Sometimes that simple gesture can give you the encouragement you need to go on with the fight.

At first I was frightened when we came to Houston. I didn't want to see so many people that were ill. I think I wanted to hide from it and pretend that it didn't exist. I think a lot of people feel that way until they are confronted with it. Now I look at the hospital as a place of "HOPE."

90

Where would any of us be without that? I see that hope in the eyes of so many people every single day. The hope that their treatments will be successful; the hope that a remission will last. *The hope for a cure.*

We are all taking a journey that is unfamiliar to us, one that can lead us to places we don't want to go. I have learned that my faith is growing with each step I take. At times I even allow myself to rest in the knowledge that God is leading our journey and no matter where it takes us, we will never be alone. I haven't gotten perfect at submitting it all to God, but I'm working on it. A dear friend sent me an e-mail with a little thought for the day attached. It went like this: *"No matter how bad the storm, God is in your boat."* (Thank you, Dave Potts, for reminding me of that.)

I was working on a jigsaw puzzle one evening while George was watching TV. He was sitting in his recliner and I had a clear view of him from where I was sitting. Every once in a while I would catch a glimpse of him with his hand on his head. This went on for a while and finally I got up to see what he was doing. There on the end table next to his chair, was a pile of his hair. He had been sitting there pulling it out in little tufts. He had discovered that his hair was beginning to come out from the chemo. We weren't expecting this until after the next round of chemo but we could see it had already started. I said "Let's just finish the job" and I went to get my clippers!

It was Saturday, October 30, and we decided we needed a *date night*. George's counts were back up and we wanted to celebrate. The next round of chemo would be starting in another week and we wanted to do something together before then. We chose a movie because that took the least amount of energy for George. He had been having a few twinges in his lower back all day, but he insisted that he felt good enough to go out. Halfway through the movie I noticed that he was shifting around a lot in his seat. I asked

God is in the Details

him if he was OK and he said he was. A while later I asked him again and he said, "My back is bothering me a little." I thought we should leave but he wanted to stay.

When the movie was over and we were leaving the theater, I noticed that he was having trouble walking. I asked him how bad the pain was and he said, "I'm OK, it's getting better." It didn't look like it was getting better to me so I suggested a trip to ER. He was NOT having any part of that and said he would feel better when he got home and could lie down. We got almost home before he said to me, "On second thought, maybe we had better head over to the hospital after all."

By the time I got him out of the car and into ER he said his pain level had gone from a 6 to a 10+. For once the ER wasn't crowded and I was relieved to think he could be seen right away. I asked the nurse at the desk if there was a place that George could lie down because he was in such pain and it was worse when he was sitting. She said they would see him in just a minute. At one point he decided that if they didn't take him to a room with a bed he was going to lie down right in the middle of the waiting room floor! After a third attempt to convince this woman that he needed attention NOW, she finally came around the desk and asked us to follow her inside.

They got him in bed but there was no getting him comfortable. He couldn't lie still for the pain. When the doctor came in he said that he was ordering IV fluids and that they would draw some blood. (Everywhere he went, they wanted to draw more blood.) They were checking for a kidney problem at first. The pain was so unbearable that I begged the doctor to give him something for pain before the lab reports came back. They gave him morphine through his IV and finally the pain started to ease up but it was still bad.

When the lab reports were back the doctor came back

in the room. He said that everything checked out just fine and that this pain was probably caused by the Neupogen shots. This was the first time we had heard of this side effect; I was relieved that it wasn't serious, but I was upset that no one had told us to expect this. The doctor told us that bone pain is the most common complaint from people receiving Neupogen but that in George's case, his was more severe than normal. They had already given him two doses of morphine by the time they released him to go home. I still don't know how I was able to get him to the car that night. He was full of pain medication but he was still able to walk.

It was after midnight when we got home. Before we went to bed he was to take two pain pills. I couldn't believe how much pain medication he was able to tolerate and still he was in pain. He was finally able to go to sleep but I lay there for hours. The party animals next door were in full swing!

By morning the pain was almost gone. I had decided to go shopping for a birthday gift for myself. My birthday was the next day and George hadn't been able to shop so he told me to go buy something nice that I wanted. I wasn't gone long before I found a cute leather jacket that I loved. It would be just about the right weight for winter and I hadn't brought any sort of jacket with me when we moved to Houston. I was happy with my purchase and knew that George would be relieved that I had found something that I liked so well. Even if he had been well enough to shop, he hated shopping! We had been planning to go out for dinner to celebrate my sixtieth birthday but I really didn't think it would be much fun if George wasn't feeling up to it. He kept insisting that he wanted to go, but this time I wasn't going to give in. Chemo was in four days and he needed to be ready for that. Birthdays come every year and this year mine didn't seem all that important.

I hadn't been home for long when the doorbell rang.

God is in the Details

When I opened the door there stood a delivery man with the most beautiful vase of flowers in his hand. George had managed to surprise me; my sixtieth birthday turned out to be special after all.

Seven

·· ❦ ··

November 4. Chemo day (Cycle B). What a frustrating day this turned out to be. We waited until almost 7 p.m. for the call from the hospital. I was stressed, but then I was *always* stressed on chemo day. As hard as I tried, I couldn't get past the worry of another round of chemo. It terrified me. I think I just knew too much about the drugs he was going to get. I had read and re-read those lists of side effects until I had them permanently engrained in my memory. I could never be content to just know "a little," I had to know everything there was to know. He had an easy time the first round, but we had already been warned that Cycle B could be worse. He would be getting ARA-C this time around, which is Cytarabine with Methotrexate added. This was a harsh combination and I was already dreading it.

It was so late when they got George settled into bed that I knew it was going to be a very late start to chemo. I kissed him good night and left to go home about ten.

God is in the Details

I walked in the house and noticed how cold it was. The temperatures had been on the chilly side for the past few days, so I had turned on the heat before we left for the hospital. I went to check the thermostat and it was fifty-six degrees in the house! That was cold for Houston! The switch was on, but the furnace wasn't working. I went to call the landlord, but of course all I got was an answering machine. I left him a message and got ready for bed.

I had seen the cars lining the street and could hear the party next door before I got to the bedroom. This time they had a bonfire going that lit up my entire bedroom like a neon sign. I opened the blinds and could see that it was a Halloween party going on, complete with costumes. The patio table was stacked with empty beer bottles and the doors to the house were wide open. People were inside, outside, and down the driveway. The music was vibrating the windows, and as usual, the dogs were joining in the fun. I knew it was going to be a very long night.

I went to bed and turned on the portable fan to *high*, hoping to drown out some of the noise. That didn't help so I just lay there trying to decide what I wanted to do. I thought about calling the police but decided against that. I wanted to get dressed and go over there to complain, but had second thoughts about that. I was a woman alone in the house and I wasn't sure what I might encounter if I went knocking on their door. The only logical thing I could come up with was to call the landlord, AGAIN.

This time his wife answered the phone. She told me that Randy (our landlord) was out for the evening and she asked if she could take a message. I told her to listen as I opened the window and held the phone outside. I said "Do you hear that? That's what I have to listen to at least once or twice a week. I have told Randy about this time and time again and he does nothing about it. I just got home from the hospital where my husband is in treatment for cancer and I'm tired and I need some sleep." I knew this wasn't her fault; in fact, she probably didn't even know who I was. It occurred to me that I might be better off if I told her who I was that was calling!!! Before I hung up I told her to tell Randy that I wasn't dealing with this another night and that I would be looking for another place to live. It was 5:30 a.m. before the last of the partiers left and I still hadn't been to sleep.

Daylight couldn't come soon enough for me. I had made a decision while I was lying in bed listening to the party go on all night. By 8:30 I had started looking for a place to move. We had only one dog now, so that should improve our options. I put Buddy in the car with me and we headed to McDonald's because I was in desperate need of an extra large coffee.

I drove through the neighborhood street by street just as I had when I was first looking for a house to rent. I came home with a short list of phone numbers to call, but no one would even talk to me without a year's lease. I wasn't about to give up; *I was on a mission.* I just went to Plan B. I remembered one of the apartments that we had looked at before we rented this house. It was one that George and I both liked and it wasn't far from this house. In fact it was even closer to the hospital.

I didn't want to put this all on George's shoulders so I decided not to say anything to him until I had something definite to tell him. I wasn't ready to tell him that we were moving! I called George to see how chemo was going and told him only about the furnace not working. I wasn't ready to go to the hospital yet because I had to go look at the apartment first. I just made up the excuse that I had to wait for a service man to come out to look at the furnace.

I went to the apartment complex and spoke with the rental agent. She showed me a book that had pictures of the different floor plans they had available. I told her I needed

God is in the Details

a two-bedroom, two-bath apartment, preferably on the ground floor. Oh, and I needed to move in on Monday! She had several units available but only two on the ground floor. She showed them both to me and I decided on the spot to take one. By 1 p.m. I had rented an apartment, called the utilities to have our service transferred, and had found a local mover to move all our things on Monday morning. I couldn't believe it...*I had accomplished all of that in less than five hours.* Now all I had to do was break the news to George that he would be coming home to new surroundings on Monday. (And one more little detail; I had to pack the whole house and have it ready to move in two days!)

It all hit me at once and I found myself sitting in the middle of the kitchen floor bawling my eyes out. I had never done anything so impulsive in my life. I was praying that I had made the right decision, but it was too late to back out now.

I got to the hospital a little after two. I had put on my "hospital face" before I walked into George's room. The first thing he asked was if the guy had come to check the furnace. I had completely forgotten about the furnace! I didn't want to lie to him but I didn't know how to break the news. I just blurted it out. "Oh by the way, we're moving."

The look on his face was priceless! I didn't get a verbal response right away but I knew it was coming. "We're WHAT?"

I started talking so fast that he didn't have a chance to say a word. I told him about the all-night party, and what I had told the landlord's wife. I was sure that he wasn't going to be able to get any rest at home because obviously Randy wasn't going to do anything about the parties next door. I stopped just long enough to take a breath and then went on to explain about the apartment and how nice it was and

98

how quiet it had seemed when I had walked through the complex that morning. I was running out of things to say and finally when he got the chance to say something, all he said was, "Do whatever you need to do." That was it. (It was a lot easier than I thought.)

I did my best to assure him that I could handle the whole move and that he didn't have to think about anything but getting through the next couple of days. I didn't dare let him know how overwhelmed I really was. *How in the world was I going to pack this whole house and have it ready for movers by 8:00 on Monday morning?*

I didn't stay at the hospital very long at all. I had to go home and start packing but I told George to call me if he needed anything because I wouldn't be going anywhere except home to pack.

I had just started packing some of the things in the kitchen when a service man showed up to check the furnace. Randy had never returned my phone call, not even to say he would send someone over about the furnace. The guy wasn't there very long at all. No one had ever bothered to light the pilot light on the furnace and that's why I had no heat. Actually, I didn't even need the furnace anymore. I was radiating enough of my own heat just thinking about packing all those boxes.

I had managed to get things packed quite easily for the move to Houston, but I had come with a lot less than I had now. I had groceries that I didn't have before, plus we had bought some things that we needed when we got there. It was surprising to me just how many extras we had accumulated in such a short time. I didn't have time to think about that, I just needed to keep packing boxes.

I had been packing non-stop for several hours when I thought about the mail. I had forgotten to stop to check the mailbox. We had several nice cards from people that I wanted to make sure I took with me to the hospital the next

God is in the Details

day; besides the cards there was a small package addressed to me. It was a "birthday package" from a friend of mine in Michigan. Diane had been diagnosed with lung cancer at the same time George was diagnosed with lymphoma. I had gotten to know her when I had taken her a book one day. She writes a human interest column for our hometown newspaper on Fridays and I always followed her articles. She had written about her cancer diagnosis and all the emotions she had gone through when she had heard the word *cancer.* One Friday after I had read her column, I had the sudden urge to take her a copy of a book that I had just read. It had helped me so much when we found out George had cancer and I wanted to share it with her. Once I read the book, I had ordered several copies to keep on hand just for times like this.

I remember driving to her house and knocking on her door. She came to the door with a puzzled look on her face. She just knew I was going to try to sell her something! I introduced myself and told her why I was there. She invited me to come in and we sat on her front porch and talked for a long time. Before I left we hugged and I handed her the book. I told her that I believed that God had sent me there so that I could meet her and give her that little book. *Now God was using her in my time of need.*

Inside the package was a lovely note, a few pieces of Great Lakes Chocolates that I love, some hot chocolate mix, and a few little bags of herbal tea. Next I came across a little picture frame that was really a magnet. The frame had a picture of flowers and a saying written on it. It simply said, "GOD IS IN THE DETAILS." She would never know how much that magnet meant to me. (Thank you so much, Diane.) I was in such turmoil and felt that I was in this *huge* mess with no one to help me, and I admit, I was feeling pretty depressed right about then. This was the perfect gift for me. I needed this reminder that, God *does care.* So many times we convince ourselves that He only listens to the BIG things we pray about, but that wonderful little magnet reminded me that He is there in *every* detail of our lives. I knew that He had this move all planned out for me. He had given us this house when we needed it, and now, he had supplied another place for us. *I just needed to be reminded,* that's all. I remembered something else then. "When God closes a door He opens a window." I had such a sweet sense of peace. Suddenly I found more energy than I could have imagined. I packed into the wee hours of the morning humming hymns to myself the whole time.

I ran to the hospital for a quick visit the next morning. I couldn't wait to tell George about my perfect gift and I needed to tell him how very much I loved him. Day two of chemo had brought no problems so I felt comfortable leaving him. I knew he was in good hands.

I never heard a word from the landlord. I had written him a letter and put it in the mail explaining the reasons we were moving. I told him how much I appreciated the fact that he had rented the house to us when we needed it. I really hated to leave because we liked the house, but my first concern was for my husband. He needed a quiet place to come home to. I asked him to return our security deposit but I didn't really expect him to. ($1750 is a lot of deposit!) I packed all weekend and even managed several trips to the hospital to see about George. I worked day and night and still had energy to spare. I was able to have everything packed and ready for the movers by 8 a.m. Monday just as planned.

The movers arrived late, but then I expected that. Late was the key word for my life. Everything was always late; *except God.* He always had perfect timing! The move was completed in about three hours and the furniture was all in place and the beds were set up for me. All I needed to do was unpack a few things in the bathroom and find the sheets

God is in the Details

and blankets to make our bed. I had taken one last walk through the house to make sure that I had left everything in perfect condition and as I was leaving I put the key on the kitchen counter. As I walked from room to room I felt my eyes fill with tears. I felt a kind of sadness when I closed the door for the last time. We had a lot of memories there. Some were good and some were bittersweet, but I had a connection to that house. I couldn't help but feel as though I had left part of me behind.

When I took Buddy to the apartment for the first time, we went for a walk around the area where people could walk their pets. This opened up a whole new horizon for him. He smelled and sniffed every square inch of the place. He had never been anywhere that had quite so many new and interesting things to explore. There were a lot of dogs at the complex and he had already started making some new "friends." I was hoping this would help him adjust to his new surroundings. He developed an instant friendship with a cute little Italian greyhound down the hall named Radar. He also discovered what cats were all about when he had his first encounter with one that didn't want to become "*close*" friends. All in all, that first day was exciting for Bud.

I picked George up that same day around three in the afternoon. He was feeling really good and had no problems so far. On our way out of the hospital we passed Norm's room and stopped in to see how things were going for him. He wasn't as lucky as George had been and was having severe nausea and was running a fever. They had stopped his chemo for awhile to give his body time to recover. He was hoping that he was going to be able to finish the round. He had gone into the hospital two days before George and would probably be there a few more days. I felt so blessed; George was handling chemo very well.

Buddy was at the door when we got home, ready to

welcome George. There were boxes everywhere but I had made a nice wide path around everything so that he could get to his recliner. He said he liked the apartment so far, and immediately noticed that it was indeed *quiet*.

It took Buddy a few days to adjust to apartment living. He didn't understand that he couldn't just bark whenever he wanted to. There were noises that he wasn't used to and that would set him off. The first night, the smoke alarm in the bedroom went off about 2 a.m. for no apparent reason. He flew up off the bed and under the bed he went. It took a lot of coaxing to get him to come out. I had just gotten him settled down and wouldn't you know it...*the alarm went off in the living room.* I tried everything I could to get that one to stop and finally I just climbed up on a chair and hit it with my broom. *That worked.* Buddy decided that he much preferred "under" the bed so that's where he stayed for the rest of the night. I could tell that apartment living was going to take some getting used to for all three of us. The one bright spot that I could see was that there were no loud parties going on!

I was tired. In fact I was very tired. All the packing and moving were catching up with me. I still had the whole apartment to organize, but that was going to have to take a backseat to the daily trips to the hospital that were starting again. George's fatigue was really bad this time and I found him sleeping in the chair every time I came into the living room. His appetite was pretty good, but he had to be awfully careful about what he ate. His blood sugar was sky high and the insulin wasn't making much difference. I was giving him his insulin shots every day and I was proud of myself for the "technique" that I had developed. Just when I was convinced that I had become a pro at giving shots, George told me in no uncertain terms that I wasn't good at it, "*at all.*" I tried to find the humor in that, but somehow it escaped me.

God is in the Details

His counts had bottomed out already and so had his potassium. When we went to the clinic they ordered something called a "baby bottle" from the pharmacy and when I went to pick it up, it looked *exactly* like a baby bottle. We had to take it to the infusion department so they could hook it up to his CVC. He carried it around under his shirt and they let us go home with it that way. The infusion was to last for three hours and when it was empty, they had shown me how to disconnect it and clean the area. He came home that day with his "baby bottle" and wearing his "duck mask." Now that was a *Kodak moment* if I ever saw one!

The mouth sores had started to appear. The rinse they had given him for that seemed to help, but food wasn't tasting good at all. He had a sore on his arm and a raw spot on his elbow. He had experienced a few minor nose bleeds and now was having some trouble with his eyes. I knew from reading that awful list of side effects that the ARA-C could cause conjunctivitis. I called the clinic and they prescribed an ointment for the raw sores and some drops for his eyes. We were told to keep a close watch on the nose bleeds and if they should get any worse we were to go to ER. I think I knew everyone in the ER on a first name basis by this time. George didn't even want to hear "ER." He thought he had made too many visits there already.

We called Norm at the hospital to see how he was doing and he told us he would be there a few more days. He had a bad rash, similar to what was on George's arm, but his was a lot worse. His hemoglobin was very low and they were going to give him a blood transfusion before he would be ready to go home. I was hoping nothing worse was about to happen to George.

I e-mailed Jay to see how he was doing after his ARA-C round. He is another online friend that I met on my website. He is from Pennsylvania and had come to MDA for his second opinion but had chosen to have his treatments done at the University of Pennsylvania. Jay was having some of the same problems. In his case his nose bleeds were severe and he had to have a platelet transfusion. He said that worked wonders for him and that he was still "hanging in there." A few days later we learned that Jay had actually been admitted to the hospital for a few days because his counts were so low. I just kept praying that this wasn't going to happen to George.

The dreaded bone pain began on the seventh day. This time we started the pain medications as soon as George felt that first twinge. By the next morning, however, he could hardly stand up and felt dizzy. The dizziness was another side effect. Along with the dizziness came the nausea. I gave him some of his nausea medicine and more pain medication for the bone pain and he spent most of the day in his chair. He was hardly able to function all day. We were going to the clinic the next day and hopefully his counts would be up and he wouldn't have to take the last three Neupogen shots.

I got so tired of watching what he had to go through. I couldn't do anything to help him except to just "be there." He told me all the time that he couldn't do it without me, but that didn't help the way I felt at times. I wished I could have done something more for him. I wished I could have taken part of his pain so that he wouldn't have had so much to bear. My kids always told me that I was strong and that I could get though it, but I wasn't strong. Whatever strength I had was from God. If it weren't for Him I would have given up a long time ago. I didn't have what it took to go through what George went through. I really didn't. I just had to depend on God for it all. God gave me little things all the time to remind me that He was with me. That day it was a verse that says, "In our weakness, His strength is made perfect." I was beginning to have those little verses and sayings written everywhere. On the days

God is in the Details

that my spirits were low, I would pick up something and find one of those little reminders written in places that I didn't remember writing them. *God never fails me.*

One night I had gone into Target to get a few things that I needed, and I noticed a man sitting on a stack of boxes. He immediately reminded me of George. He was bald and wearing a cap, his duck mask, and a pair of latex gloves. I recognized him as a cancer patient with low blood counts. I smiled at him and said, "Taking a rest, are ya?" He smiled back at me and said, "Yea, I'm about worn out, but my wife is still running the aisles somewhere." About that time his wife rounded the corner and we started a conversation.

I told them about George having lymphoma and that we had moved to Houston for treatment. They had come from Arkansas in June. His name was Al and he had just finished chemo and was waiting for a bone marrow transplant. He had AML, a deadly form of leukemia and he was sixty-six years old, the same age as George. They said they were Christians and I told them we were too. We stood there in the middle of the aisle at Target and shared all that God was doing in our lives. *God brings people together at certain times for a reason.* He had brought the three of us together to encourage one another and to remind us once again that He is truly "The Blessed Controller of All Things." (I first heard that phrase at a woman's seminar years ago and wrote it down in one of those places that I had forgotten about until just recently.) This was to become a very important reminder to me in the days and weeks to come. No matter what our situation, God is in control.

It still amazes me at how well our bodies were designed by God. If I hadn't known it before, I know it now. I see it everyday. Our bodies are strong, stronger than we know. We can survive things beyond our imagination and still live to tell about it. I will never understand how anyone could *ever* doubt that we are a creation of God!

On Thursday, we had the usual clinic visit. George's white cell counts were back up so he was able to "unmask" again; however, his red cell counts were quite low. They gave him a Procrit shot this time, which acts on red blood cells in the same way that Neupogen works to increase white blood cells. His platelets were low as well, but not yet to the point that he would need a transfusion. He was feeling lousy this time around. The dizziness and nausea were still with him and all he was able to eat that night was pudding. Nothing else appealed to him and he was afraid that he wasn't even going to be able to keep the pudding down. He was complaining about his eyes hurting and his vision being blurry. He stayed cold all the time and I'm sure that too was from chemo. (We can blame almost anything on chemo.)

I was thinking about how cold it must be getting in Michigan and appreciating the fact that we were somewhere nice and warm for the winter. The milder weather really made it a lot easier for all the trips we had to make to the hospital. I thanked God everyday that MD Anderson wasn't somewhere in the frozen north!

George had been talking about taking a little road trip one of these days. There are a couple of military collectors that he knows that are within a couple of hours of Houston. He was itching to pay them a visit. I saw that as a good sign! If he was thinking about doing something that he loves, then maybe improvement was just around the corner. We had thought about going up that way over the weekend, but he was just not up to par. He decided that he would rather wait until a better time when he would be able to really enjoy the trip. I was glad that he decided not to go. I was tired and it seemed as though I never got everything done that I needed to do between chemo treatments.

Thanksgiving was just around the corner. This was a year of "firsts" for our family. It would be the first holiday

God is in the Details

that George and I had spent alone but I couldn't help but reflect on all the things we had to be thankful for this year. I knew I would be lonesome for our kids and it was hard to think of being alone for the holidays, but we were here and this was where God wanted us. We were in Houston for George's treatments, but I also knew that God was using his cancer for the plans He had for my life as well. I was growing in my faith by leaps and bounds and my life had become about so much more than the "*things*" I had always treasured. My heart had changed, although I knew that His work in me was far from finished. Sometimes God takes us away from those things that interfere with His plan, and puts us where He can work best in our life. In Houston I had to depend on Him for everything. I had accepted that and my job was to do as that old saying said, "I was to bloom where I was planted."

Buddy and I were taking a walk one day and he *introduced* me to Radar's "daddy." (Radar was that sweet little Italian greyhound that Buddy had noticed the first day we moved to the apartment.) Brad and his wife, Judi, lived just down the hall from us. I was tickled to have met some nice people to talk to once in awhile. George wasn't always up to listening to my endless chatter and I found myself talking things over with Buddy on more than one occasion. Of course Buddy was always agreeable, and everything I decided was OK with him as long as I took him to McDonald's whenever I stopped there for coffee. He loved sticking his head out the window to enjoy all the delicious smells. He had discovered that he really liked the taste of their coffee creamers so I always ordered an extra one just for him. He would sit in his spot in the back seat and watch every move I made when I opened the lid and started to stir the cream into my coffee. He would wait very patiently and when the time was right, he would climb over the seat and wait for me to open his. I knew

108

that I was spoiling him rotten, but he repaid me with his sweet disposition and his boundless enthusiasm whenever I came through the door. He was great company for me while George was in the hospital.

Thanksgiving Day was the following day and we had a visitor coming! My best friend, Betty, was coming from Michigan for a few days to spend the holiday with us. I couldn't wait to see her. I knew she would lighten the mood around our apartment if anyone could. We had been friends for more years than I could count. I had been baking pies for the past two days and you would have thought I was expecting a whole group of people, but I wanted everything to be perfect. It was going to be late when she arrived so George went to bed and I sat up to wait for her.

It was almost midnight before she got to the apartment but I wasn't ready to go to sleep! We talked for a long time until I finally took pity on her and let her go to bed. I knew she was tired from her trip, but I could have stayed up all night talking and never gotten tired. I found that I was starved for some "girl talk" and I planned to get my fill as long as she was there. I was already feeling sorry for George because I knew he wasn't going to be able to get a word in edgewise between Betty and me. If there was anything the two of us girls could do, it was talk and shop!

And shopping we did. We tackled every shop in the area and then decided to head to the Galleria. To say this was a large mall was an understatement. All the big name stores are located there, most of which were way too expensive for our budget, but it was fun to "window" shop. Mostly, we talked. And talked. And talked. There is just *nothing* like a girlfriend.

By the time we got back to the apartment, George was starving. I was glad to see that he had his appetite back so

God is in the Details

we headed to our favorite spot for dinner. (Yes, we went to the Salt Grass!) Betty loved it as much as we did. George couldn't believe that we still had things left to talk about, but talk we did. Once in a while we even let him join in on our conversation! We all ate way too much as usual, but we had a wonderful time. The days were passing much too quickly for me and in no time Betty was going to leave. I wasn't ready to see her go, and I was even less ready for round three of chemo to begin.

Eight

· · ❦ · ·

Two days before chemo was scheduled to begin, George was scheduled for x-rays and CT scans. They would be doing these routinely after every two treatments to give the doctors some idea how the chemo was working. We had one day between testing and admission to the hospital so we tried to rest and get ourselves prepared physically and mentally.

We met with Dr H the day chemo was to begin. He was very pleased when he told us the results of the tests. The node near George's clavicle was now half the size it was, but the *best* news was that there were no nodes left in his neck. He told George that he was pleasantly surprised by how well he was tolerating the chemo so far and then said, "I think I should make George our poster boy for the lymphoma clinic!" He was thrilled by the progress, but not nearly as thrilled as we were. The news was better than either of us had expected and it made George even more anxious to get going with round three. We went straight from there to admitting and George had a room in no time.

God is in the Details

The next day I wasn't able to go to the hospital. I woke up early and was feeling very ill. I was so dizzy that I could hardly walk and there was no way I was going to attempt to drive. I wasn't sure if I had a "bug" or if it was a new medication that I was taking that was causing my problem. My doctor had put me on an antidepressant just a few days prior because she felt I was depressed. Me, depressed? *Yes, I was depressed.* No matter how hard I tried to talk myself out of it, no matter how much I tried to give it all to God, I was *still* depressed. I felt guilty because I was weak. I was under the misguided impression that Christians aren't supposed to get depressed. I'm not sure where that thinking came from, but that's exactly what I was thinking.

I slept off and on all day. Buddy was very cooperative and only asked to go out when it was absolutely necessary. He was more than content to lie on the bed with me all day while I tried to sleep. I couldn't help but feel that I should be able to get myself together and take care of everything like I always did. I had a million things I needed to be doing and lying in bed wasn't on my list. I needed to be with George and here I was, dissolved into a heap of depression.

I had finally gotten to the point of despair and just cried my heart out to God. I didn't want to be like this. I wanted to be strong and able and I was neither. Sometime during the night I got a sense of well-being. I didn't feel quite so worthless and I actually felt as though things would work themselves out for me. When I went to bed I wasn't sure that I was going to keep taking my medication, but by morning I had decided that it wasn't a sin to need help once in a while. I didn't see myself as weak, I just saw myself as very vulnerable, and very *human*. I knew that God was going to give me grace for the day, and then tomorrow He would give me more. Two lines from a hymn were going through my mind as I woke up that morning: "*He giveth more Grace as our burdens grow greater; He sendeth more Strength*

112

as our labors increase." That was all the assurance I needed.

George was now on his third day of chemo. This was Cycle A and I wasn't expecting too many things to go wrong. After this treatment, he would be at the halfway point. When I got to the hospital he had already been up walking the halls. The steroids were again causing extreme swelling and when I saw him I told him he reminded me a little of the *"Pillsbury Dough Boy."* I ending up massaging his feet and legs the whole time I was there. They felt like water balloons that were ready to pop. I could see he was already tired of being in the hospital. He was bored with TV, bored with eating, and tired of being in bed. On the positive side, his vision had cleared up and Dr H said that it was from the Methotrexate.

This round was totally uneventful and George was able to come home on the sixth day. Nothing was out of the ordinary and so we would begin our normal routine that we always followed after chemo. Labs, Fast Track and all that came with it.

About a week after chemo, his counts were down as usual. Fatigue was becoming a constant companion and he was spending more and more time napping in his chair. He knew he would be coming home with his mask on, so he decided to take up a little hobby. When he was feeling up to it he would paint little faces on his mask or write something across the nose of it. This week it said "Jesus Saves." He would do anything to cheer up the people he saw at the clinic when he went in for his visits. He never failed to elicit someone's comment or at least get a smile or a big *"thumbs up."*

People really responded to George. He has a lot of charisma and an upbeat personality that people like about him. He is always ready with a joke or a quick comment to lift someone's spirit. *I know that God is using this as a ministry.* Even the nurses looked forward to seeing him. They would tell him that no matter how their day was

God is in the Details

going, they always felt better when he walked through the door. He was my hero through all of it. I tried to tell him that often because he needed encouragement just as much as those he tried to encourage. He even told me that my job was harder than his, but I wasn't buying that for a minute. It takes a special kind of person to go through what he was going through. I was just the bystander and the cheering squad.

(At our church in Michigan everyone calls him "The Candy Man." He makes it a point to shake hands with everyone who comes into church on Sunday morning, even the babies. When they shake his hand, he puts a piece of candy in theirs. It's his way of welcoming them into God's house.)

Our friend Jay and his wife, Linda, came to Houston for Jay's check-up that week. We were going to meet for lunch and George and I were really looking forward to it. I was excited to finally be able to put a face to the name. I only wished that Norm and his wife had been here to join us, but after round two he had gone back home to Abilene to finish his last four treatments.

We picked them up at their hotel and headed to Salt Grass. (Of course) That place couldn't be beat as far as we were concerned. There were other restaurants we enjoyed going to, but this was tops in our book. What great people Jay and Linda are. We talked for over two hours and we hated to end our time together, but they had to get back to their hotel. I already knew that we would love them both even before we met because of all the e-mails we had shared over the past few months. When we dropped them back at their hotel, I knew that we would remain friends long after chemo. I had come to think of George, Jay, and Norm as "The Three Musketeers." They were all going through chemo at the same time and were always there to talk each other through the tough times. Friendships that are made in times like these are like no other. They are formed by sharing our deepest fears and are nurtured by encouragement and hope.

Christmas was just a week away by this time and we were awaiting the arrival of our daughter Shelley and our granddaughter Elizabeth. They were coming to spend a week with us and George and I could hardly wait. It had been four months since we had seen either of them and I wanted everything in the apartment to look festive. I bought a small table-top tree and decorated it. I even strung lights around the counter between the living room and kitchen to give the apartment that Christmas "feeling." Nostalgia had already set in. Christmas had always been my favorite time of the year, a time I cherished because our family was always together. How different it was this year. There would be no family celebration, no big dinner to share together, no gifts to open around the tree, and no candlelight Christmas Eve service at our church. I was going to miss all that, but I wasn't going to let anything spoil the small celebration that I was planning with the girls. We were going to be together and celebrate the true meaning of the season.

I had tried to prepare the girls for how George looked now. He had lost a lot of weight and of course all his hair. (Even those hated nose hairs were gone.) He was very pale these days and he looked sick. He looked just like all the other cancer patients that we saw every day. We had gotten used to the changes as they happened, but this was going to be hard on the girls when they saw him for the first time. I was more than a little concerned about the effect it would have on Elizabeth especially. She was thirteen and very sensitive. All I could do was hope that I had prepared them well.

Their plane was late. Late was something to be expected but I was upset because they didn't get to the apartment

God is in the Details

until after midnight. George had already gone to bed. He tried his best to wait up for them, but the fatigue got the best of him. When they got there they were both tired, so after a bunch of hugs and kisses I sent them to bed.

I was surprised that I fell asleep as soon as my head hit the pillow. I must have been more tired than I realized.

The girls were so happy to see George the next morning. Elizabeth kept telling him that he looked handsome without any hair! I think that cheered him up a lot. I had either done a great job of preparing her or she did a greater job of pretending. Either way, everyone was in great spirits.

After breakfast Elizabeth wanted to open Christmas presents. I was glad because I wanted to make sure that everything we had bought for them fit so we would have time to makes exchanges if we needed to. Of course, Elizabeth's leather jacket that I bought her was too small. I realized how much she had grown in only a little over four months. They both loved their gifts but that jacket had to go back. We stayed home in the evening and the girls and I played cards. It seemed like forever since I had seen those girls. I knew that I had missed my family, but I didn't realize just how much until that moment. I couldn't stop looking at them. It was as though I were drinking it all in and trying to etch it in my mind. I wasn't sure how long it would be before I saw them again and I was already dreading the time they would have to leave.

Elizabeth was so excited to be in Houston and naturally she wanted to go to the Galleria. That was the second and last time that I would go there. I got such a kick out of watching those girls at that mall. Shelley was thirty-eight and wasn't all that impressed; shopping wasn't a top priority to her, but Elizabeth was a different story. She made the whole trip fun by just watching her reactions to all the top name stores. She just *had* to go into Neiman Marcus to *touch* a Prada shoe! I had forgotten how impressionable thirteen-year-old girls can be. We ended up in Macy's and I bought them each a bottle of perfume and one for myself. Our shopping trip ended there and home we went.

We took the girls out to dinner that night but George hadn't told me that the bone pain was starting. This time it was in his hip instead of his lower back. He told me he had taken a pain pill earlier but it wasn't working very well. He managed to sit through the entire meal without ever letting the girls know he was in pain. He didn't want to spoil their fun so he kept it to himself. That is why he managed the chemo so well; he was stubborn and refused to let it get the best of him. He coped with things as they came and didn't think too far ahead; he didn't worry about things before they happened. I can't tell you how many times I wished I could be like that.

I was glad when we got home and I could give George some more pain medication and get him on the heating pad. He decided not to tell the girls he was feeling so bad and just went straight to bed.

The next day the girls wanted to go swimming. I laughed myself silly at the idea. It was 70 degrees at most and just because the sun was shining and they were in *Houston,* they thought they had to go in the pool. I decided that the best way to handle that situation was to do nothing. I walked them to the pool area and gave them the code to get in. I had offered to give Elizabeth one of George's heavy terry robes to use when she got out of the water, but she refused. She insisted that she wasn't going to need it. About the time Shelley's big toe touched the "ice" water, she gave up on the idea of a swim. Elizabeth, on the other hand, was a bit braver. She lowered herself slowly into the water until it was just above her waist before she changed her mind. She shivered all the way back to the apartment and wished more than once that

God is in the Details

she had taken that nice warm robe when it was offered to her. We got a good laugh out of that, but she insisted that she was going home to tell all of her friends that she had been *swimming* in Houston at Christmas.

The time flew by, just as I had known it would. Soon it was time for my girls to leave. We had arranged to have them picked up early on the morning of Christmas Eve. I would have liked to keep them there until after Christmas but I knew they needed to be with their own family. Saying good-bye to them was harder than I had expected. I tried my best not to cry and I actually held back the tears until the limo had pulled out of view.

When they got to the airport, Shelley called to tell me that their plane was delayed and that they would have an extra two hours before they would be leaving. Before they were to land in Cincinnati, their connecting flight was canceled. A snowstorm had hit the East Coast and flights everywhere were canceled. Their luggage had been diverted to Atlanta for some unknown reason, and they were stuck at the airport. Shelley was tired and Elizabeth was scared. People were sleeping on the floor at the airport and hotels were filling up fast. Shelley had no credit card so she couldn't book a hotel room even if they could find one. I tried calling different hotels to use my credit card to book them a room but none of them would accept it over the phone. They were going to take people on a first-come basis and only those who had an actual credit card with them. I decided to call our son because he has a way of getting things done when no one else can and sure enough he used his *persuasion* and booked them a room. Shelley had enough cash with her for a cab so they were able to get to the hotel.

Christmas Day in Houston was beautiful. It had turned cold over the past couple of days and during the night it had dropped down to 20 degrees. We woke up to snow

118

covering the grass and shrubbery around the apartments. I couldn't believe we had *snow*. I got up right away because I wanted to take Buddy for a walk and enjoy the crisp air and the sound of the snow crunching beneath my feet. We walked around the entire complex; neither of us was in a hurry to go back inside. I couldn't help but think about the kids. I knew that their holiday was different this year too. Our house was the "gathering place" and everyone had always looked forward to coming home for Christmas. I had hoped that they would all make it a point to get together even though Dad and I weren't there, but they hadn't. They were all going their separate ways for the holiday and that left me with a sad heart. I thought about "next year" and wondered what we would all be doing then; would we all be together? I didn't want to think sad thoughts; after all, it was a day too special for sadness. It was Jesus' birthday and I wanted to focus on that.

I wasn't the only one out that early walking their dog. Everyone was talking about the snow and no one could ever remember having snow in Houston for Christmas. I simply told them all that I had arranged it as a Christmas gift from me. The high for the day was 42 degrees, but in a couple of days the temperatures would be back in the 60s.

When Buddy and I got back to our apartment I had a message on the answering machine from Shelley. I quickly called her back to find out how their night at the hotel had gone and to see what time their flight would be. She told me that all the flights to and from Cincinnati had been canceled for the day, and possibly for the next day as well. I had a moment of panic wondering what those girls would do. I knew their money was almost gone and they had no luggage! Shelley calmed me down by telling me that James was driving there to pick them up! I knew that was at least a five-hour drive in good weather and there was no way of knowing what the driving conditions would be. I hated

God is in the Details

it when my kids were out on bad roads. They were all grown and in their thirties but they would always be my "kids." Christmas Day was certainly not turning out the way any of us had planned but if I had learned anything at all during the last year, it was that "plans" are always subject to change.

George and I took it easy all day. We were both feeling a bit melancholy and we already missed the girls. Their call came very late that evening saying that they were all home safe and to wish us a Merry Christmas. I was so glad to get that phone call. They had been on my mind all day and it was a relief to know that all was well.

Monday morning it was 65 degrees and a bright sunny day in Houston. You would never have guessed that the ground had been white with snow just a day before. George and I decided to take that little road trip that we had been saving for a *better* time and today was it. We drove to College Station, Texas, which is about a hundred miles from Houston. George had been waiting patiently for the day to come when he felt up to making the trip. With the next round of chemo starting in just a few days, it was now or never. He had known the guy we were going to see for years, and he couldn't wait to get there and poke around in all his "junk."

I had been doing all the driving since we moved to Houston and I was still not too sure about the expressways. There are expressways everywhere and it's hard to go anywhere without having to drive on at least one of them; surprisingly, the drive turned out to be a nice experience. Traffic was light once we left the city and the countryside was beautiful.

The place we went to was nothing more than a field of vehicles in all stages of repair or *disrepair* as the case may be. There were parts in buildings, lying in the yard, and stacked in piles. It was the usual junkyard variety, just the kind that George loved. It had been raining there for over a week, and every spot that didn't have something sitting in it, was full of mud puddles. I wasn't about to get out of the car with Buddy, so he and I took a nap while George explored. I was happy to see him enjoying the day so much. He spent hours digging through all that stuff. He is a die-hard collector who never misses an opportunity to look for some hidden treasure.

George had owned his own business for years, mainly dealing in military vehicles/parts. We have an office in our home and a warehouse on our property. I knew it was hard for him to be away from the work he enjoyed and this little trip had been really good for him. When he got in the car after spending the day rummaging around in all that "stuff," I could see the wheels turning. He was already thinking of some deal that he would be making in the next few months!

I took Buddy for a walk when we got home. We took the trash out and then stopped at the mailbox. I took a quick look through the mail and noticed a letter that had a Houston postmark but no return address. That piqued my interest so I opened it first. There was a check from our previous landlord in the amount of $1750; he had returned our security deposit in full! The check was the only thing in the envelope; he had sent no note with the check. I couldn't wait to show it to George! What a perfect ending to a perfect day.

Nine

··⚬··

It was now December 30, and the fourth round of chemo was to begin. We had the usual morning that we had every time George started chemo. We would go to the lab for blood work and then two hours later we would see the doctor. It was always the same, nothing ever changed, not even the amount of time we had to wait for his room. It was 7 p.m. when the call came. George's room was ready so off we went. I had already decided that I wasn't going to wait around for the infusion to begin because we already knew it could be after midnight. I left him at the hospital and went home to an empty apartment and one lonely little dog.

Day two was New Year's Eve. I was a little disappointed that chemo fell on a holiday this time, but it was important that the treatments follow a precise schedule. So whether it was New Year's Eve or not, we followed the plan.

George called me to say that the first infusion was finished and he was feeling good as usual. They wouldn't be starting the next drug until later on in the day, so I decided to stay home for a while and try to take a nap. I was having a hard time sleeping and hoped that a nap might help. I went in to lie down and a million things started going through my head, things that I thought I needed to be doing. That was always a big problem for me; my mind would never rest. Finally I gave up on the idea and decided to go to the grocery store. I knew what George would like to eat when he got home and I wanted to be sure that I was stocked up. This being the dreaded ARA-C round of chemo, I wanted to be ready in case there was a problem. Dr H had already warned us that this round would probably prove to be the most difficult one so far.

The hospital had planned a special evening for the patients and their spouses that night as they usually did on special occasions. They had taken reservations for dinner and I was looking forward to a little celebration even though it would be in George's hospital room. Our dinner was arranged for 7:00 but I was going early since I hadn't seen him all day. I got there around 5:00.

When I entered the room, I went over to his bed to give him a kiss. I noticed that he looked really worn out and pale but when I asked him how he felt, he said, "I'm feeling okay." I knew he didn't always tell me the truth about how he really felt because he didn't want me to worry any more than I already did. I think most people who love each other spend a lot of time in the "protecting" mode. George didn't want to worry me; I didn't want him to know just how really worried I was, so we just kept to our script and continued to act as though we had everything under control. I'm not sure that all that protecting was really good for either of us; at least it wasn't for me. There were times that I would have loved to drop my guard and be able to really talk about everything that I felt, but instead, *we talked about everything else.*

God is in the Details

Promptly at 7:00 the waiter brought our dinner. Everything looked great. We even got a white linen table cloth and napkins this time. We sat at the small table near the window, me on one side, George and his chemo pole on the other. It was impossible to ignore the fact that we were in that hospital room with those bags of chemo hanging next to us, but we were going to give it our best shot. Tomorrow would be the first day of a brand new year, and with that new year came the hope of a remission and an end to cancer for what we hoped would be many years to come.

The food was fabulous. There's no way anyone would have believed that it was "hospital food." They served spinach salad, steak, stuffed shrimp, broccoli, *real* mashed potatoes, dinner rolls, and coffee. For dessert we had chocolate mousse pie that was out of this world. We were both stuffed but we had managed to eat every bite.

After dinner we talked about what we had done the year before on New Year's Eve. We had brought my dad home from the hospital that night and I could still remember the ride home. It was snowing so hard we could barely see the road. (Had that only been a year ago?) When I thought back to that night, I hadn't known that in six short weeks I would lose my dad. He had suffered a ruptured brain aneurysm and had lived through it. At the time, I felt that he would have been better off if he had died immediately rather than having to live through those last six weeks. Dad was so ill and I had stayed at his bedside day and night, only leaving him to grab a few short hours of sleep now and then. It had been a very difficult time but in the end I knew that God had planned it all perfectly. I had found a deeper love for my dad than I ever knew existed. During those long hours that I sat with him, I felt that unexplainable love growing within me. No words can explain the range of emotions I felt at that time; I had a lot of things to settle before I was ready to say good-bye to him. I knew that God had given me the extra time I needed to rid myself of some deep-rooted issues that I had carried around in me since childhood.

Now here I sat, on yet another New Year's Eve, watching my husband fighting a battle for his life, and I was overwhelmed with some of the same emotions I had experienced with my dad. "If I could have this much love in *me*, then how much greater must God's love be for us?" It didn't matter what our situation was right then. We weren't in it alone; we had the COMFORTER with us. He was right there beside me, giving me more peace than I had thought possible. We didn't know what lay ahead, but for now, we had everything we needed.

By Sunday, things weren't looking good. George was experiencing some nausea and was running a temperature of 103. When I called him that morning, he told me not to come to the hospital. That wasn't like him; he always looked forward to my visits. Today just wasn't a good day at all. He wanted to sleep if he could and just didn't feel like having company. I had never thought of myself as "company," so I was more than a little concerned. I tried to find something to do around the apartment, but I couldn't convince myself that I should stay home. Finally I decided that I was going to the hospital and check things out for myself.

When I walked into his room, it was dark. He had pulled the shades and was asleep. I walked over to his bed and put my face next to his. *He was burning up.* I went to find a nurse to see what she could tell me. I asked if the doctor had been in yet that morning. (Weekends at MDA were about the same as at most hospitals. Doctors need time off just like everyone else and you never know when they will make their rounds.) She said that one of the doctors on the lymphoma team had already been in and said that this

God is in the Details

fever was most likely caused by the chemo. They had added more fluids to his IV along with medication to reduce the fever. I kept thinking to myself, "He still has two more rounds of chemo to go!" I was praying that this wasn't a sign of things to come.

I went back into the room and found George awake. He said he felt awful and all he could do was sleep. I decided that was probably the best thing for him so I left and went back home. I called the nurses' station several times that evening to check on him and each time she told me he was asleep.

His temperature was down to 100 by the next morning and they were still planning to send him home later that day. His last bag of chemo was almost finished and then they would wait and do a blood test. If the Methotrexate levels were acceptable, all we had to do was wait for discharge orders. He wasn't feeling all that great, but he wanted to go home.

Buddy and I went to pick him up at 3:00. He told me not to use the parking garage and that he would just meet us downstairs in the patient pick-up area. When Buddy saw him through the window that tail started wagging non-stop and over into the front seat he went. He wanted to make sure that "Dad" knew how much he had been missed.

I made sure that George was settled in and had everything he needed and I headed to the pharmacy. I had the usual ten prescriptions to fill and knew there would be a little wait. When I finally got back, we decided to celebrate with pizza for dinner. Even Buddy loved the idea; he got to eat the crust!

By Tuesday the fever was gone but the fatigue had already set in. That was still the major problem with chemo. I could see how he struggled with it and no amount of rest ever seemed to help. When his counts started dropping the fatigue level increased. He hardly ever complained about how he felt and my admiration for him grew daily along with the satisfaction that I felt in being able to take care of him and to encourage him to keep going. We made a great team, but there were days when I didn't feel as "valuable" as he said I was. I knew that was because I got a bit overwhelmed at times by everything that was required of me. *There was always so much to do* just to keep everything running smoothly. Whenever I was down, God found a way to pull me up again. There were so many times that I looked at that little magnet on the fridge and it reminded me that "God is in the details!" Some days it was those little "details' that almost sent me over the edge, but that precious magnet was always there, telling me that I had someone who would manage it all, if I would only allow Him to.

My desk was piled high with e-mails that I had printed for George to read. He always looked forward to mail of any kind. Hardly a day went by that he didn't have mail from someone. I thought that once we had been gone for awhile, people would stop writing as much, but that never happened; they were faithful. We even got "artwork" from some of the kids' Sunday school classes at our church. They drew little pictures and wrote the sweetest notes. Their spelling was that of young children and it always made us laugh when we saw how they sounded out their words. That artwork received a very special place in our hearts. Children have a way of touching us when no one else can do the job nearly as well! I had already filled up one box with all those treasures and could see that we would probably have another one full by the time we went home.

I loved e-mail! It made my job so much easier because I could type one update and send it to everyone at the same time. There were plenty of days that I just didn't have the energy to reply to everyone personally. I also appreciated having an answering machine. I could screen our calls and not have to talk to anyone when I didn't want to. It wasn't the fact that I didn't want to talk to people; it was just too emotionally draining at times. I wanted to be able to

God is in the Details

report the "good news" and not have to sound depressed when I talked to anyone. Our kids were already worried enough about their dad and about me as well. They were well aware of the fact that I had it all on my shoulders and I never wanted them to know how really bad it got at times. I knew it was important to take care of myself but George had to come first. His needs were much greater than mine, and I used my energy to make sure that he had nothing to do but get well.

Tuesday we had to go to the lab and then George had a cardiology appointment. The doctor told us that George's heart sounded great and that he was releasing him as a patient. *We needed some good news!* I was still worried about how chemo might be affecting his heart, but as the doctor said, "You have to weigh the benefits against the risks." We had known the risks when we started, but the hope for a complete remission was still our goal. God knew those same risks and He had brought us to Houston to MD Anderson. We knew that He could just have easily chosen to cure George without chemo, but instead He wanted us to make this journey. All He really expected was for us to have faith and be willing!

Walking a journey like the one we were on was probably the hardest thing either of us had ever done. We are human and that makes us vulnerable. George got discouraged and I got depressed about a lot of things. Our human nature was forever present and at times blocked out everything else but our "situation," and the fact that we were always exhausted made us even more vulnerable. It's not possible to go through something like this and always be on top. There were many dark days for us, many times we felt like we would never see the end, and I can tell you with complete honesty that if it weren't for God leading us, we would never have made it this far.

Next we went to Fast Track. George's white cell count

had bottomed out at .6. This was *not* good. We expected the counts to drop, but not so far and so fast. His red cell count was low as well. *No wonder the fatigue was so bad this time.* There was no mention of a transfusion so he just got the usual shots of Neupogen and Procrit along with a reminder to come back in two days so that they could check his counts again. On the way out the door, the nurse handed him a nice new mask. (I couldn't wait to see what he would write on this one.) He could be heard quacking as we stepped into the elevator.

We were expecting our grandson, Bret, for a visit. He would be here in just a couple of days. Bret's mother, Rose, is George's daughter by a previous marriage. I consider her *one of my own* since we have been a family for thirty years. Where do I even begin to tell you about Rose? She has cancer too. Her cancer is rather rare and is called carcinoid. This is a very slow-growing type of cancer but sometimes carcinoid syndrome accompanies the cancer itself. Unfortunately for Rose, she has that as well. It's this syndrome that causes her a great deal of discomfort and pain. The medication Interferon that she takes causes its own set of side effects such as chills, fever, and joint and muscle aches, similar to a bad case of the flu.

Rose and her husband, Dan, are raising three boys. Bret is the oldest, and is almost twenty-one. Justin and Ethan are both in high school. If that weren't a big enough job, Rose works as a surgery tech for a dermatologist in the Chicago area. She just never gives up and never gives in. She wants to be more than what cancer wants her to be and as she says, "If I give cancer the attention it wants, then I will become nothing but cancer." She is, without a doubt, the strongest person I know. When I see George and his strength and the determination he has, his positive attitude through all he has been through, I see Rose. They are both survivors.

God is in the Details

Bret arrived on Saturday. George was feeling good and was happy to see his grandson. They started making plans for the things they would be doing during the week. I wasn't quite as optimistic as they were, because I knew that George's counts were low and I wasn't sure if they were going to rebound soon enough for him to actually be able to get out and do things with Bret. I didn't want to be a wet blanket so I just listened to them talk.

Bret slept late on Sunday. George and I were lazy as well and we decided not to do much that day. When we had gone to Fast Track for the last appointment, the counts were still low but we were hoping they would be coming up by the time we went back again on Tuesday so the guys could get on with the plans they were making. George wanted to take Bret up to College Station with him so the two of them could rummage through military parts again. Bret was excited to go and I was excited *not* to go! I was really hoping for the best and knew it would be good for George to have some *"guy time"* for a change. By evening my fears had started to come true.

George was running a slight fever. It wasn't high and he told me he was fine, but I knew that this could be the beginning of a problem. He had just completed Cycle B and I had been preparing for trouble. He looked worn out to me, but I knew he was trying his best not to give in to it.

His temperature was 100.7 by morning. Even he had to admit that he wasn't feeling all that great. I called ER but they told me just to give him some Tylenol unless the temperature reached 102. (For some reason, 102 is the magic number.) Everyone is assumed to be OK unless their temp is 102. I will never understand that because I know how sick I can be without having a temp that high. This time the Tylenol seemed to work its magic and the temp went down to 99.2. George was thrilled; I was concerned. He looked bad to me. I had seen fatigue before, but this

130

seemed to be more than just fatigue. To make matters worse, I had just received an e-mail from Jay's wife, Linda, telling us that Jay had been admitted to the hospital for fever, fatigue, and low blood counts. "Great, just what I *didn't* want to hear." I could tell from the tone of her e-mail that she was worried. She said that she was beginning to question whether or not they had made the right decision to have this aggressive chemo. I tried my best to send an encouraging reply, but I really didn't know what to say. Each of us had to make that decision on our own and I was sorry that they were having doubts. George and I talked it over and he was still convinced that we had made the right choice for him. All we could do was continue to get our strength from God and to allow Him to lead.

Whenever I thought of God leading me, I remembered something that I had read a long time ago. The Civil War was raging throughout our country and Pastor Joseph Gilmore of the First Baptist Church in Philadelphia wanted his congregation to take their eyes off the war and turn them toward God. He knew that God was leading them no matter what the situation was at the time. That afternoon, after he had preached his message, he wrote the words to the hymn "He Leadeth Me." The chorus ran through my mind.

He leadeth me, He leadeth me
By His own hand, He leadeth me
His faithful follower I would be
For by His Hand He leadeth me

I was willing to allow God to lead me. I wasn't sure where we were going, but I knew He held my hand.

Later in the day, Bret and I went to get some ice cream. George had been napping in his chair for a long time, or so I thought. He was actually just lying there with his eyes closed, not wanting to talk. He said he just felt sick and was trying to sleep but couldn't. I thought maybe the ice

God is in the Details

cream would perk him up just a little, but it didn't have the effect I had hoped for. When we got back, I found him in a rather serious mood.

He wanted to tell me how much I meant to him and how he appreciated everything I was doing for him. I was beginning to get the feeling that something was seriously wrong. This reminded me of the way he had acted the night before his heart surgery. He had said basically the same things to me that night as well. This was scaring me. If George was worried, then I was doubly worried.

I wanted to go to ER right then, but he refused to go. He insisted that he would be OK until morning and then we would go for our usual appointment at Fast Track. I wasn't at all comfortable waiting till morning, but he said he was going to bed. I went in a little later and checked on him; he was sleeping. I stood there for a few minutes just enjoying the peaceful look on his face as he slept. I was trying to convince myself that he would be just fine by morning, but when I crawled into bed beside him, I wasn't so sure.

Tuesday morning was January 11. We got up early to go to the lab and to our Fast Track appointment. George was still running a slight temperature but the thing that was causing me the most alarm was the way he looked. His eyes were glassy and he had absolutely no color to his face. I was glad that we were going into the clinic so they could take a look at him.

We had a bit of a walk to the garage at our apartment and I couldn't help but notice that George wasn't all that steady on his feet. I was holding onto his arm and every once in awhile I noticed him hesitate just a little. We finally got to our car and I asked him if he was OK. "I'll be OK" was all he would say. He was quiet all the way to the hospital. I knew we were going to have a two-hour wait after the lab and suggested that we come home to wait. He

132

said he would rather just wait there because it was too hard on him to make two trips. When we got to the parking garage at the hospital I got out of the car first and started to look around for a wheelchair. When he realized what I was up to he said, "I'll walk." I didn't know why he had such an aversion to wheelchairs but when I thought about it, I think it was because that was a sign that he was too sick to make it on his own, and he wasn't going to give in to that idea. He was stubborn, sometimes to a fault!

Well, walk we did! It was a very long walk to the lab, but he was determined that he was strong enough to make it. After we got finished at the lab, we still had another walk to get to Fast Track. Again, he said, "I'll walk."

I knew it was going to be a long wait at Fast Track the minute I saw how many people were in the waiting area. I had no idea how many of them were ahead of us so I asked the receptionist if I could talk to the nurse. I never minded waiting our turn, but that day was an exception. I wasn't sure what was going on with George, but I knew it was serious. When she came out I told her that George was really ill and asked if we could be seen as soon as the lab report came back. She was the nurse that we saw most times and she had a soft spot for George. He always gave her a hard time and always had a joke to pull on her. She always looked forward to seeing him. She assured me that she would put a "rush" on the labs and would call us just as soon as she could.

George was sitting in a chair with his head back and his eyes closed. He would hardly answer me when I would talk to him. The wait seemed to go on and on until finally the nurse was calling his name. We got back to the exam room and she took one look at him and said, "Mr. Pretty, you really are sick, aren't you?" Then she had to give us the bad news; they were admitting him to the hospital! She had already spoken to Dr H and he had decided that from

God is in the Details

what the lab reports indicated, it was too dangerous to treat George outside the hospital. (I knew it; I had known something serious was going on.)

He couldn't be admitted to the hospital from Fast Track, so we had to go to ER. We were at the opposite end of the building from where ER is located, and this time I wasn't taking no for an answer. I asked the nurse for a wheelchair.

They took George straight to a room when we arrived in ER. I just assumed that the nurse or the doctor had called to say we were on our way since we didn't even have to stop in the waiting room; we were whisked through the door the minute we got there. The first thing they did was to start an IV and draw some blood. Next they came in to tell me they were taking him to radiology for a chest x-ray. While he was gone, I made my way out to the waiting room searching for a coffee pot. We had been at the hospital for a few hours by this time, and I hadn't eaten since very early that morning. I poured myself a cup of coffee and then called to let Bret know where we were. After that I found a chair and sat down.

A lady was sitting in the chair next to me and asked me who I was in ER with. I told her I was there with my husband. She could tell I was a little upset and had heard some of my conversation with Bret on the phone. She reached over and squeezed my hand and told me she would pray for him. That started a conversation and she proceeded to tell me about herself. She was in the final stages of metastatic breast cancer and had come to the ER because she was having a severe reaction to a medication. I looked down at her hands and they were covered in red blotches that resembled burns. She told me that she was in a lot of pain and was hoping she could get someone in ER to help her. They had just stopped all of her cancer treatments and she was going home to die. I couldn't believe that she was so calm as we sat there talking. She told me that she was at peace about dying and that she was ready to meet God. What a testimony this woman had. There she sat, ministering to me, and she was the one who was dying. I hated to leave her there alone and I was wondering where her family was. I asked if someone was there with her and all she did was shake her head and say, "God is all I have." I hugged her before I left and told her that I would be praying for her.

They were just bringing George back from his x-ray when I walked through the door. He wasn't even coherent by this time. He looked deathly ill and all I wanted to do was cry. He wouldn't respond to me when I tried to talk to him; all he did was lie there not moving. He wouldn't open his eyes; he wouldn't respond when the nurse asked him questions. *I thought he was dying.* His skin felt so hot and dry and his temperature kept going up. I had never seen him like this and I was frantic. I knew that I had to get myself under control because he needed me, but I didn't know if I could. Then I thought of the woman in the next room and I decided that if she could face dying, then I could find the strength I needed to help George. I knew that God had placed her there for me.

It was as though time stood still in that tiny ER room. I started praying and asking God to speak to me and let me know that He was really there. Scriptures kept coming to mind, the first of which was "Be still and know that I am God." I knew that I needed to release George into God's care. I stood next to the bed and held onto George's hand and told him that I loved him and *I asked him not to leave me.* I prayed and I cried; I reached out to God in every way I knew how. When I ran out of scriptures that I could remember, I started repeating the words of hymns that kept coming to mind. *Then I started talking to the devil.*

I had a few things that I needed to say to him. I knew that

God is in the Details

he would like nothing better than to destroy the closeness that I had with God and he was going to do his best to defeat me. He didn't want me to find peace; *he wanted to watch me suffer.* I spoke out loud. I said, "George belongs to God and He alone will decide what happens in this room." I told him that he wasn't going to win this time because I wasn't going to allow it. I would sing praises all night if I had to but satan wasn't going to win the battle. (I refuse to capitalize the word satan; he isn't worthy of the importance that signifies.)

It never occurred to me until later that the door had been open the whole time and anyone could have heard me. Someone could have easily walked in and found me talking out loud, but I really didn't care. I had a score to settle and I refused to stop until God had the victory.

It was 9:30 that night before they moved George to a regular room. He was still unresponsive for the most part and the doctor on duty that night told me that George was a very sick man. I planned to spend the night at the hospital, but the nurse wanted me to go home. She said that nothing good would come out of my staying up all night and she promised to call me if anything happened. I knew she was right; I needed to try to get some rest because I had no idea what I could be facing by morning. She gave me a direct number I could call at anytime during the night and check on his condition. I still didn't want to leave him but I knew that I had given him over to God and he was in good hands. I forced myself to go home. Bret had been home alone all day and I knew he would be glad to see me.

Poor Bret. He had come all the way to Houston, expecting to spend time with his grandpa, and he had ended up dog-sitting! He was still awake when I walked in. Buddy had met me at the door thinking I was home to take him for a walk, and Bret had questions about George.

136

Diane Pretty

I told him everything that had happened and that I would be calling the hospital several times throughout the night. I promised that I would wake him up if anything changed.

I looked down at Buddy, his tail wagging in anticipation of a late night excursion, and I didn't have the heart to disappoint him. I put his leash on and we went out for a walk. The night air was cool and refreshing after being in the hospital all day and it felt wonderful. I stared at the stars and thought about how God must have decided exactly where to place each one. It was the same way that He had chosen where to place me. I was in the exact spot where I was supposed to be and He was going to make me into something He could use. He wasn't doing this to make me suffer; He loved me enough to know what was best for me. All He expected from me was my total trust.

Dr H was worried when I saw him at the hospital the next morning. George's counts were about as low as they could go and his temperature was staying around 104. They were giving him antibiotics through his IV every eight hours but it was too soon to tell if they were going to work. Cultures had been taken to see if they could find any kind of infection, but we wouldn't know the results from them for another day or so. George was barely aware of his surroundings and very ill. The doctor had ordered two units of blood to have on stand-by because he knew they would have to do a transfusion soon. Once the hemoglobin dropped under 8, they would be ready for the blood. In the meantime they were going to give him a transfusion of platelets because his platelet count was down to 11,000. Dr H said, "Things aren't looking too good right now." Before he left the room, he came over to where I was sitting and put his hand on my shoulder. When I looked up at him, I could see the distress in his eyes. I knew that when a doctor was that concerned, it was serious. He told me that it was *very* serious and that

God is in the Details

the next few days would be critical.

I sat as close to the bed as I dared. Even though they hadn't quarantined the room, they didn't want me to go too near the bed and I wasn't allowed to touch George at all. His immune system was so compromised that they didn't want him to come in contact with anything that might be on my hands or clothing. I sat there for awhile just watching him breathe. I didn't know what I would do if he should die, and I didn't want to think about it. I had to keep a positive attitude because that was what George would expect me to do. He was never willing to give up and I knew that I had to encourage him even if I wasn't sure if he could hear me or not. I told him over and over that he was going to make it. He was going to fight his way through this and I was right there with him.

I had to leave for a little while and go get Bret; he wanted to see his grandpa. We came back to the hospital and sat with George for a while but he didn't really want us there. He didn't even want *me* there. All he wanted to do was lie there with his eyes closed. He said he felt too weak to open them and too weak to talk. I think our being there tired him out so we left. We stopped at the nurses' station on our way out and I gave her my cell phone number. I asked her to please call me if George asked for me or if anything changed. I wasn't comfortable leaving but I didn't want to sit in the room and disturb him either. *I felt absolutely useless.*

I took Bret out for a nice dinner. I really enjoyed having him with me. We had never had a lot of time together, one on one, and even though I knew that grandmothers weren't all that exciting to a college guy, Bret seemed to enjoy our time together as much as I did. I was just sorry that the week hadn't turned out as planned and I knew that when George got better he was going to be sorry that he missed quality time with his grandson.

Diane Pretty

I kept thinking about "when" George got better not "if." I refused to believe that he was going to die.

The next day was January 13 and it was Thursday. They were giving George two units of blood when I got to the hospital, and his counts were still at critical levels. His platelets were only 64,000 even after the platelet transfusion the day before. I got to see Dr H when he made his rounds and he said that George's bone marrow needed to "wake up" and start making neutrophils, which are part of the white blood cells that protect the body against infection. With his counts so low, the bone marrow wasn't doing its job. Unless things changed, George was in danger from all sorts of infections which could be fatal. His temperature was still hovering between 102 and 104 and there had been no improvement at all so far. We needed a miracle and I was trusting God; after all, He is the one that is in the "miracle business."

On Friday as I was leaving the apartment on my way to the hospital, I asked God to speak to me. There had been so many days with no change in George's condition and I was getting discouraged. I got in the car and turned on the radio. I hardly ever listened to the radio and really didn't even know what stations were on in Houston. I just hit the "On" button and the first thing I heard was a man asking, "Do you trust God in all areas of your life?" My radio was tuned in to a Christian station that I knew I had never listened to before, but there it was.

The speaker's message that day was on faith. He went on to say how easy it is to say we have faith when everything is going well in our lives, but the true test comes when we are in a crisis. "This is when we make the choice to fall apart and blame God for our situation, or trust Him with the outcome." I had known that when I asked God to speak to me He would do just that; I just hadn't realized it was going to be quite that *clear.* God had been speaking

God is in the Details

to me for months in one way or another but this particular day it really pierced my heart. He was telling me that it wasn't important *what* my situation was at the time, but how I handled the situation that mattered. I knew right then that George was going to get well. I couldn't explain it other than to say that I just *knew* it. I stopped worrying. I wasn't sure when things were going to change; I just knew that God had given me the assurance that they would.

When I got to the hospital, I found George lying there with his eyes closed just the way I always found him when I got to his room. When I spoke to him he opened his eyes and attempted to smile at me. I could see the discouragement in his eyes and I knew he felt like he was never going to get better. I started telling him how God had spoken to me in that radio message and that I felt such peace. I told him that I knew that he was going to be OK. I wanted so much for him to feel the same excitement that I felt, but I knew that wasn't possible; I also knew that I had to encourage him to believe it.

The doctor came in shortly after that with the news that there had still been no change according to the lab reports that he had seen earlier. He was going to add yet another antibiotic to the IV and told us that they were covering all the bases and treating every kind of infection they could think of. He was even having someone from the infusion department come up to the room and check for any sign of infection in and around the CVC site. When he left I couldn't help but think, "He said there had been no change, but I know better." God was about to change everything!

As the afternoon passed, George started improving. Maybe not by lab test standards, but I could see it! He talked to Bret and me more than he had all week and by evening he wanted something to eat. His temperature was going down and by the time we left it was almost normal. I almost danced all the way to the parking garage and I already knew that by morning the news was going to be good.

Bret had to leave Houston early on Saturday morning. I was sorry to see him go because he had been such good company for me all week. I called for the limo to pick him up and gave them his departure time, not once realizing that I was looking at the wrong flight! By the time he got to the airport he had five minutes to catch his plane! I felt so bad about the mix-up and was glad he was young and had the energy to run through the whole airport! I waited at the apartment until he called me to let me know that he was actually on the plane and then I hurried to the hospital.

I had just gotten to George's room when Dr H walked through the door. This time he came in with a huge smile on his face. "He turned the corner and his counts are coming up!" When he said those words I think that was the instant that I fell in love with our doctor! I knew he had been worried about George all week thinking that he was in for a major problem. The look of relief on the doctor's face was the most welcomed sight I had seen in a long time, except of course, for the identical look on my husband's face. I couldn't believe it when I heard George say, "Does that mean I can go home?" I was hearing that from the man who only hours before had been too weak to speak and now he wanted to go home!

I could tell that Dr H was seriously considering his reply. He had paused for a few minutes before he said, "I'm tempted to let you go today, but I think another twenty-four hours without any complications would be a better decision." He told George that he needed to get out of bed a few times during the day and walk around the room, and if he felt up to it he could start walking in the hall the next morning. He said he would see how things were by morning and before he left he promised to discharge him

God is in the Details

the next day if he was up to going home.

George couldn't get out of that bed soon enough. He was weak and it took a lot of effort, but he was determined. I helped him up and we walked to the bathroom door and back to the bed. It was about five feet to the door but he said it felt like a mile. I had my doubts as to whether he would make it out to the hall by morning, but I had learned not to take anything for granted. God had lifted him from near death, and I wasn't going to limit what else He had planned. I was just so grateful that we have a God who answers prayer.

He was walking in the hall the next morning, unassisted, and I brought him home at noon! *Miracles do happen*, and not just in books. I had seen a miracle with my own eyes and vowed never to doubt the power of God in my life.

Ten

·· ☙ ··

If we had needed just one more thing to happen, I found it. I had gone to see a dermatologist about a spot I had on my nose. I had been a bit concerned about it for some time, but kept putting off having it checked. It was just a little dry patch on the side of my nose and sometimes it would get a little scab on it. It wasn't painful, didn't itch, but it would bleed if I happened to wash over it just a little too hard with the washcloth. It had been there for a couple of years but I had noticed that it had changed. I was a little suspicious so I wasn't really surprised when the doctor said he was going to do a biopsy.

He told me he would have the results in a few days and that he would let me know if I needed to come back.

I was really hoping for good news, but I was not able to convince myself that this was "nothing." I think I knew it was some kind of skin cancer all along, but didn't want to admit it. I didn't have long to wait for my answer

When the doctor's office called me, they asked me to

God is in the Details

hold on and then the doctor came on the line. He said that the biopsy report had confirmed his suspicions and that it was a basal cell carcinoma (skin cancer). He was referring me to Dr. Nelson for a consultation and he assured me that he was one of the best in his field.

A couple of days later I went to see this Dr. Nelson. He explained to me that he would do something called MOHS surgery on my nose. This is a process where he would take a layer of tissue from my nose, examine it under a microscope to see if the margins were clear of cancer, and if not, he would repeat the process. He would keep doing this until the cancer was gone. He said it was the best way to treat the kind of skin cancer that I had and that the likelihood of it coming back was slim. He then explained how he would have to go about closing the area. The easiest way would be to stitch it closed and that would be simple. If the cancer was deeper, then he would have to use a technique called a skin flap. The worst case scenario would be a skin graft. He couldn't tell me which he would have to do until he actually did the surgery and saw what his options were. He thought I should have this done as soon as he could schedule it and I went home wondering how I was ever going to fit this into my schedule.

When I got home I must have looked a little "deflated." As soon as I closed the door George asked, "What's wrong?" I had decided to downplay the whole thing and not give him too many details. The last thing he needed was to worry about me! He had to get his strength back and have another round of chemo in just a couple of weeks. I didn't even want to think about chemo after what he had just gone through, but I knew it was coming…and now I had to decide what to do about having surgery!

I told him that I might need a little surgery but I wasn't going to have it right away. He pressed me for details, but I wasn't ready to unload on him. I just wanted some time to think about it and decide what my options were, so I called Rose. Since she assisted a dermatologist with surgeries she was the one I needed to talk to. Her boss didn't do MOHS surgeries personally but knew a lot of surgeons around Chicago that did and was going to ask if anyone knew of Dr. Nelson. Rose encouraged me to have the surgery done as soon as I could and promised to call me when she found out anything about Dr. Nelson.

Of course, my kids called to ask what I had found out at the consultation. They were adamant about me not postponing the surgery and told me that it was something that I needed to do. I still hadn't decided what to do and I knew that the next two rounds of chemo were going to get worse for George. There was just no way that I could have surgery and take care of his needs at the same time. I decided to wait.

A couple of days later, Rose called to tell me that Dr. Nelson had an excellent reputation in his field and that the dermatologist she worked for suggested that I go ahead and have him do my surgery. The timing was just all wrong. George needed me to be 100 percent when he went through his chemo. I had no one to help me in case I ended up having to have a skin graft. I came up with every excuse in the book until I picked up the phone and scheduled my surgery for February 8.

George would be finished with his fifth round of chemo by then and hopefully he wouldn't have too many problems for the first week afterward. I knew I might be cutting it close, but I was going to depend on God for the details.

I called my daughter Shelley and asked her to come to Houston to help us when I had surgery. She was happy to come and I was relieved. Some way we would make it through this.

Chemo was scheduled for January 27. The time had flown by and I could hardly believe that the time was

God is in the Details

here already. George had gone for his CT scans a few days before and we were anxious to see how everything looked after four rounds of chemo.

Dr H was so pleased with the results of the CT scans. He wouldn't use the word "remission" but he went as far as to say, "There is NO evidence of active lymphoma!" I think doctors hesitate to use the word remission at that point for fear that their patients will stop chemo too early. He had always been emphatic about the fact that there could be cells floating around in the lymphatic system that could go undetected, and it was very important to finish the whole regimen of chemotherapy.

We couldn't have been happier with the news, unless of course Dr H had said that George was "cured." We knew we would probably never hear that word since there is no cure for MCL, but we would always pray for a cure one day. We were in a great mood, especially George. His spirits had been challenged a lot lately and today he had his old enthusiasm back and his focus on the goal. He was ready to get on with it!

This time the call from the hospital didn't come until 10 p.m. We decided that I would just drop him off and come straight home. There was no telling when or "if" chemo would start that night and there was no use waiting around to find out. We had become accustomed to this routine after so long, and we had come to expect these late starts.

Friday, January 28. I called the hospital at 9 a.m. and woke George up. Chemo had finally gotten started at 3 a.m. and he had been awake until 7. Poor guy, I had no idea that his night had been so bad. I stayed home until afternoon so that he could get some sleep. I puttered around the apartment but couldn't get much accomplished. Finally I took Buddy for a long walk. The day was beautiful but a little chilly for Houston. Buddy loved the walk and so did I. I could almost forget about hospitals and chemo and nose surgery and everything else and just lose myself in the moment.

I loved Houston. I knew that I would miss it when we left but it wasn't "home." Home was where my heart was, it was where my kids were, and I wanted to be there as well. Our time here would end before we knew it and I couldn't wait for that day. I wanted to be as far away from cancer as possible. I was tired. No, I was exhausted! I never seemed to relax and all I could think about was the next appointment, the next hospital visit, or the next trip to ER. It was our routine for sure, and I was going to be very happy when it was over!

I found George in much the same mood. He was bored with TV, and that wonderful hospital food he had loved was now becoming boring as well. Mostly he was bored with being cooped up in a room and attached to a pole that he had to push wherever he went. It had been six months of hospitals for him and he was ready to see it end even more than I was.

He had called to ask if I would bring something "new" to eat when I came. I had no idea what he considered new, so I opted for a couple of taco salads. That was something that we didn't eat often, so I knew it would at least be a change. After we ate, we turned on a movie and I crawled up in bed with him and we just cuddled for a while.

I could see he was deep in thought about something. He kept talking about being cured when he got finished with chemo. I knew that he had heard the doctor say more than once that there was no cure. I didn't want to discourage him, but at the same time I didn't want him to expect something that would never happen. I was torn between giving him the *"reality check"* and risk discouraging him even more, or I could let him believe what he wanted to believe. It was a hard spot for me because I am the realist and George is the avoider. I had always thought that his

God is in the Details

motto must have been, "Avoid at all costs!" I wanted him to stay positive because he needed that to make it through the next couple of months. I finally decided to change the subject and let Dr H deal with this. I started talking about "home" and that cheered us both up.

We knew we couldn't plan an actual time when we would be able to leave Houston, but we both had our hearts set on being home for Easter. I couldn't think of a better time to be home. I wanted to be able to go to church and celebrate that day with my friends and family. Easter had always been the most important holiday that a Christian can celebrate, in my opinion. This was the time of year when we think of Jesus' death on the cross, His burial, and His resurrection. *HE GAVE HIS LIFE FOR ME!* He loved me that much; He loves *you* that much!

By Monday Dr H was getting a bit concerned about George's red cell count. He told us that he was going to order blood in case he decided to do a transfusion. George's blood sugar was going crazy again as well since this was Cycle A and he had to have the steroids again. Our friend Norm is also a diabetic and he was having the same problem as George with his blood sugar. I had just gotten another e-mail from him and he said that his chemo was delayed because his counts were still too low. As Norm had said, "Now I know what the bottom of the barrel looks like!" (I think George and Jay could sympathize; they have all been looking down into that same barrel.)

Dr H was talking about making a change to the last round of chemo. It would be the final round and another of the Cycle B, or the dreaded ARA-C. He told us that most patients have the most trouble with the last round and he would have to decide how he wanted to proceed. After what George had just gone through, I wasn't looking forward to that last round at all. Dr H thought about just repeating Cycle A again and not doing another of the

Cycle B, but was leaning more towards just reducing the dose and going ahead with the protocol. Either way, there was just one more left after this one!

I decided that we needed a treat since the news wasn't that great and even though George didn't mind getting another transfusion, I hated the idea. To me it was just another sign of complications and I didn't want *complications*! I headed downstairs to the coffee shop to get two cappuccinos.

On the way, I noticed a woman coming toward me pushing a little boy in a wheelchair. The child looked to be around six or seven years old and he was wearing the "mask" and latex gloves, signifying that he had low blood counts. I immediately smiled at them as I passed by and could hear the little boy singing! He was singing "Jesus Loves Me!" I couldn't help but be touched by this little guy! I had wanted to smile and give him encouragement when I saw him, and he ended up being the one who encouraged me. It never failed; someone was always there for me whenever I needed them. God never failed me; He was always *right on time.*

As I made my way down in the elevator, I thought about all the faces I would see, just in a small space of time. I would get off the elevator and I would see some of them. I would walk down the hall and see more…and there would be those standing in line once I got to the coffee shop. Their faces would look different, but their needs were the same. They needed hope and they needed someone to bring it to them. I wanted God to use me. I wanted to give back in some way, all that had been given to me.

When I got to the coffee shop, the line was long as it always was. I wasn't the only one who wanted a break from the hospital room and the coffee shop was a popular place. While I was waiting for the girl to bring my order, the woman behind me ordered a "French vanilla cappuccino." That was what I had ordered so I turned toward her and

God is in the Details

said, "That must be popular tonight, that's what I just ordered!" She gave me a halfhearted smile and shook her head. I could see that she was troubled but I wasn't sure if I should say anything else to her. I tried to turn away, but something in her eyes stopped me. I knew that I may be overstepping a boundary by asking but I couldn't help it. I said, "What's wrong? You look like you could use someone to talk to."

She didn't even hesitate. She told me that she had just been told by her husband's doctor that he had only days to live and she had been walking the halls trying to get herself together before she went in to see him. She was there alone and had no one to talk to. She told me that she couldn't believe that I had reached out to her just when she was at her breaking point. I stood there and talked to her for as long she needed to talk and when she was leaving she stopped and put her arms around me and said, "You'll never know how much you helped me." She was so wrong; I did know. I knew because God had sent me an angel every time I needed one.

Chemo went so well that I was almost afraid to hope that George had seen the worst. His counts had rebounded and he never had to have the transfusion. I was thrilled and amazed at the same time. His endurance never failed to astound me. The guy could be down for the count one minute and up and running the next. Now all we had to do was hope that this upturn lasted long enough for me to get through my surgery.

Shelley arrived on Sunday, February 6. It was great to see her again and I was so glad that she was able to come to be with us for the next week. I wasn't expecting my surgery to be anything more than an unwanted "bump in the road" and so I wasn't expecting to need more than a day or two at the most to recuperate.

George's bone pain had started the night before and

it was relentless as usual. This time it was lower in his leg, mostly around his knee. While he was resting, I took Shelley around the area to show her where my surgeon's office was, where the grocery store and pharmacy were located, where there were some good "take-out" places, and finally to the hospital so that she would know where to go to take George for his appointment. I kept telling her that she wouldn't have to do all this, but I was showing her "just in case." I really was planning to be up and around the day after my little surgery.

When we got home I had gotten an e-mail from Jay. He had really sent it to George. He wanted to let George know that he wasn't the only one going through this horrid fatigue so he sent along some humor. He said that he had taken a bath and it had worn him out so much that he had let the water out and had to sit there until his wife came home from work to help him out of the tub! George got a chuckle out of that and asked me to send a reply back saying that he had been so tired that morning when he got up that he had to walk around the apartment in his underwear because he had been too tired to put his pants on. Those guys could still find ways to make each other laugh! There's nothing easy about what they were going through but all three of them tried to stay positive and still find a bit of humor along the way. I admire anyone who can go through what they had and still have their outlook!

The next morning I was up early. George had to be at the lab before 7:30 and afterward we came home to eat breakfast while we waited for the Fast Track appointment. I could tell the chemo effects were already starting and I was hoping they would hold off just a few more days. When we got back to the clinic, I was right. His counts were already down and he had to wear a mask home. (He had written John 3:16 on his mask that day.) They told us that

God is in the Details

the effects of the chemo are cumulative and that with each round, the fatigue would be worse. That was certainly the case. George could hardly put one foot ahead of the other these days. The nurse seemed a bit puzzled when she took his blood pressure. In fact, she took it three or four times. Every reading was around 92/52, which was quite low for George. She phoned the doctor and he discontinued one of his heart medications that also acts to lower blood pressure. She just told us to watch for signs, such as dizziness or unusual weakness and if anything should happen to go to the ER. (George tuned that part out; he didn't want to hear anything about going to the ER.)

After Fast Track we went to the infusion department for his infusion of Vincristine and then to see a doctor about adding another type of insulin to his daily regimen. His blood sugars were still sky high so they were going to try to get a tighter control over his glucose. All this took about five hours and by the time we got home, George was more than happy to see his recliner. I couldn't believe that he was able to accomplish all that on top of suffering with the bone pain. (*He's quite the man.*)

I was having surgery at 7:00 the next morning and my day was still in full swing. I wasn't even able to think about surgery so I guess that wasn't all bad. I ran out and picked up something for dinner and brought home a prescription for Shelley. She had just had a tooth pulled a few days before and was having a problem with an infection and pain. That's all we needed...one more thing to go wrong. If that wasn't enough, we had yet another interruption.

George's blood sugar was 477 after dinner! I had given him all the insulin that was prescribed and it was still that high. I tried and tried to persuade him to go to the ER. He wasn't having any part of that! He told me that he had been in the hospital enough and wasn't about to spend another night in the ER. I can't say that I blamed him for that attitude, but this was serious business. Obviously his new insulin wasn't working as fast as we thought it would. I went into the bedroom, closed the door, and as quietly as I could, I called the ER. They told me to increase the dose of insulin by a few units and if that didn't help, I was to bring him in! When I told him what I had done, he wasn't too happy with me but he let me give him another insulin shot and then he went to bed. I finally gave in and went to bed myself, only to spend the night tossing and turning and dreading the next day.

Shelley and I got up at 5:30. She took Buddy out for his walk while I took a shower and got ready to go. I was to take a Valium at 6:00 so that I would be relaxed by the time we got to the doctor's office. Naturally Shelley had to drive and by the time we arrived, I was feeling more than a little relaxed! I wasn't sure that I was going to make it from the car to the elevator.

We got to the surgery suite around 6:50 and they called my name at precisely 7:00. They asked Shelley if she wanted to stay in the room with me for the procedure and she said she did. I was surprised that she was so brave and all I could think was, "Oh great, they'll be picking her up off the floor in no time!"

The first thing they did to me was give me some shots in and around my nose. They made my eyes tear, but they weren't all that bad, actually. As soon as my nose was numb, the doctor took his first "slice" and then his assistant cauterized the area. Nothing had been painful so far, but I really didn't like the smell of burning flesh. (Especially my own!) We waited about forty minutes before the doctor came back in and I was glad that Shelley was there to keep me company. When he came in he said that the margins weren't clear so he would have to repeat the procedure. This called for another numbing shot, another slice, and another cauterization! The assistant brought me another

God is in the Details

Valium and said, "Maybe this will help."

Forty minutes later, right on schedule the door opened and in walked Dr. Nelson. "Bad news, the margins are still not clear." He told me there was a lot of cancer left and so it went for two more times. I was beginning to wonder if I was going to have a nose left at all, when he reappeared to say, "We have clear margins!"

I was so relieved and thought, "Now all he has to do is stitch me up and I'm ready to go!" Shelley was still hanging in there with me and I was amazed that she was doing so well. Dr. Nelson sat down on the stool near my head and gave me the next bit of info...the "worst case scenario" was now my reality. The closure was going to require a skin graft. I was in NO way prepared for that. I asked him where he was going to take the graft from and he told me it would be from the very inside of the bridge of my nose, near the corner of my eye. He numbed the area, I asked for more Valium, and Shelley left the room!

I was brave! Or at least I was so looped from all the Valium that I just felt brave! The assistant took a few pictures of my nose and Dr. Nelson started the closure. He worked pretty fast and it went well. When he was done, Shelley came back in to see about me. They had asked me if I wanted to see my nose before he did the closure and I had opted to just take their word for it that I had a quarter-size hole in the side of my nose. It could have been the Grand Canyon for all I knew. I just wanted to be done and get out of there. They had the pictures that they had taken of the "before and after" and asked me if I was sure I didn't want to see them before we left. I gave in, and wished that I hadn't. I left with a huge pressure bandage on my nose that took up three quarters of my face. All I had that wasn't bandaged was part of my eyes and the tip of my chin.

Dr. Nelson gave me my instructions and I wasn't to get out of bed for the next five days unless it was to go to the

154

bathroom. I was to remain in bed and to stay as calm as possible. He told me that if I moved around too much and had any bleeding under the skin graft that it would "die" and that would require more extensive surgery. There went my plans of a speedy recovery in one day! This was a major setback for me and I needed to get my priorities straight. I needed to do exactly as the doctor ordered; I had plenty of help with Shelley there, and George didn't need to hear me complain.

I got home and settled into bed and the "feeling" started to come back. I hadn't realized just how bad it was going to hurt and I could already tell that it was going to be a long night. The doctor called me before I went to sleep just to see how I was doing and to tell me to make sure I took my pain medication. He didn't have to remind me; I was already on my second dose! He told me to put an ice pack across my bandages to help with the swelling and to expect two black eyes when I got up the next morning.

When I woke up and went into the bathroom, I hardly knew the person in the mirror. My eyes were almost swollen shut and I had bruises that I could see sticking out from beneath all the bandages. I could only imagine what I would look like once the bandages came off. I looked like I had been in a fight, and I hadn't been the winner! I was already tired of being a patient and I had four more days to go. I hated being in bed all day long but I was so thankful that I had Shelley.

George was feeling lousy. His blood sugar was still around 400 and he had another day left of the steroids. When his sugar was high, he was soooooo crabby. I knew he couldn't help it and I tried not to mention it, but it really made it hard on Shelley. She had two crabby patients and she was still trying to heal from having her tooth pulled. It seemed like the only one around that was in good shape was Buddy, and he was making the best of the situation.

God is in the Details

Poor Shelley was taking him out every time she turned around just because he knew she would! He had managed to pull the wool over her eyes and every time he wanted to go out to "investigate" he stood and looked at her until she gave in.

My second full day of bed rest brought with it a horrendous itching problem! My nose was itching so badly and there was no way I could get to it even if I dared tried to scratch it. I knew it was from the healing (or at least I hoped it was healing) but it drove me crazy. I tried not to think about it but it never seemed to let up. I wasn't in the mood to watch TV and my eyes were still too swollen for me to read...so I tried to nap as much as possible. I had thought about the luxury of spending time in bed and taking naps the whole time I had been in Houston, and now that I was forced into that situation, I found I hated it. I did NOT like to take naps. I never had and now I knew that I probably never would. I wanted to be up doing all the things that kept running around in my head and here I lay, unable to do any of it.

Shelley took George to his appointments that he had scheduled for the day. He came home wearing a "baby bottle" again because his potassium and magnesium were low. When the nurse had connected it to his CVC she had noticed that the tubing had pulled out where it was inserted into his chest so she added a couple of stitches to try to hold it in place. That CVC had to stay put until George was completely done with his chemo. He received so much chemo at one time that they wouldn't be able to use the veins in his arms and if the CVC should come out, it would have to be reinserted. I didn't even want to think about it.

While they were gone, I began to feel "guilty" for having had surgery. I knew it couldn't be helped but that didn't change the way I felt about it. I was still afraid that

156

something might happen to George and I wouldn't be able to take care of him. I knew that Shelley could handle about anything that actually happened, but it was my nature to worry about the things that "*never*" happened. I was always thinking ahead and that got me into trouble. I had to back up and remember who was in charge! I was running ahead of God instead of letting Him lead. That was a lesson that I found the hardest to learn. I certainly had enough "reminders" along the way, but I still failed miserably at times. I knew this was going to be the thing that I would have to work on for the rest of my life. I would never get it perfect, but I knew that God would keep sending out those reminders, and hopefully I *would* improve as time went on.

Another thing that I had been thinking about was an old saying that I loved. It went like this: "*Yesterday is history, tomorrow is a mystery, and today is a gift; that's why it's called The Present.*" More often than not these days, I was finding so much truth in those words. I was learning that the past was just that, *the past*. Tomorrow will come and with it a whole new set of circumstances, but *today* is that gift that has been given to each of us to open as we choose. We can moan and groan and complain that this wasn't the gift that we had expected or the gift that we wanted, and perhaps miss a blessing that was in store for us; or we can look forward to it with anticipation and decide that we are going to use every minute of the day (our gift) doing what God wants us to do.

It was the fifth day after surgery and I decided that if I didn't get up for at least ten minutes I was going to be forever attached to the bed. My back was killing me from being in bed for so long and I was sure that if I was a very good girl and only sat at the computer for ten minutes I would be just fine. I needed something to take my mind off the constant itching; I was sure it would drive me crazy by the time the

God is in the Details

bandages came off. So to the computer I went.

An e-mail from Jay was waiting for me. I couldn't even respond right away because I didn't know what to say to him. He told me that his doctor had diagnosed him with interstitial pulmonary fibrosis, or at least that was what it appeared to be. They were doing more tests to make sure. This is a lung disease that begins with inflammation and results in deep scarring of the air sacs and surrounding tissues of the lungs. It can be fatal. The doctors suspect that it was caused by one of the chemo drugs that Jay had been receiving. We were planning to celebrate the end of chemo in just a couple of months, and now he wasn't sure that he would even be able to finish the chemo. He said that this disease can have a rapid progression and he was already planning ahead to prepare things financially for his family. I couldn't believe this!

This hit me hard and I didn't even begin to know how I was going to tell George. As much as I wanted to protect him, I knew there was no way that was going to be possible. He would ask me if I had heard from Norm or Jay and I would have to tell him.

I walked into the living room and handed him the e-mail. I just looked at his expression as he read it, and I knew that his reaction was the same as mine. When he asked me if I had answered it, I said no. What was I to say?

I finally managed to write a response. I searched my heart for the right things to say. I knew that nothing I said would change a thing, but I wanted Jay and Linda to know that we cared deeply about what happened to Jay. I began the letter by telling him to make sure he found a specialist that would treat him like he was "living" and not like he was dying! I didn't want him to lose hope and I certainly didn't want him to give up! I knew firsthand about the power of prayer and I wanted him to know that I was going to pray for him. I reminded him that God performs miracles all the time.

158

Diane Pretty

Every time we see the sunrise, or a rainbow, hear a bird sing, or kiss a newborn baby...*we are witnessing a miracle.* I wanted a miracle for Jay. No matter what road we walk in this life, God has already walked it before us, making a path for us to follow. I wanted Jay to *believe* that God was going to work a miracle in his life. I told him that God always gives us grace at the exact moment we need it...and the real beauty of grace is that there is not a limited supply!

I felt I needed to say so much more. I wasn't sure what Jay's beliefs about God were, but I knew what mine were. I believed every word that I had written to him and I knew that God loved Jay just as much as He loved me. All I could do was ask God to be real in his life and to bring him strength and comfort in the days ahead.

Sunday, Shelley left for the airport. I couldn't believe that the driver was late picking her up. "Oh, here we go again!" I had hoped that this trip was going to be uneventful for her, but it didn't look promising. She barely made her flight and when she landed in Chicago, her connecting flight into South Bend had been canceled. They were able to get her on a later flight, which entailed only an extra two-hour wait. She wasn't too upset because she said, "At least we aren't in the middle of another snowstorm!"

Buddy started missing her the minute she was out the door. He stayed by the door all morning hoping she was coming back! I knew just how he felt; we were both sad.

Mid-morning someone knocked on the door and when I answered it, there was a delivery man holding a beautiful vase of flowers. George had ordered the flowers for me for Valentine's Day. I couldn't believe they made deliveries on Sunday, but there they were. George knew that the next day would be a busy one for us and that we wouldn't be home for much of the day so he wanted the flowers delivered a day early! I think he had a "double" reason for sending me flowers that day. He knew how sad I was going to be when Shelley left and he knew that the flowers would brighten my day.

He was restless all that night and kept waking me up moving around on the bed. At one point I asked him what was wrong and all he said was "I'm wringing wet." I took that to mean he was too warm and asked him if he wanted me to turn on the fan. He said he would be OK and went back to sleep. The next thing I knew, he was out of bed taking off his t-shirt. I was half asleep and so I thought he was still too warm so I reached over, turned on the fan, and went back to sleep.

The next morning I got up and walked into the bathroom. From where I was standing I had a full view of the bed. George was just waking up and as he turned back the blanket on the bed, *I saw blood.* I ran over to the bed to see where the blood was coming from. I asked him what was wrong and why he was bleeding and he had no idea. He hadn't even seen the blood at that point. I flipped back the blanket and saw more blood on the sheet. I couldn't believe how much blood there was and it was *everywhere.* It was then that I noticed the t-shirt that he had taken off in the night; it was on the nightstand and it was soaked in blood. He had thought he was sweating but it wasn't sweat, it was blood. This whole scene reminded me of a horror movie where someone had gotten stabbed or shot in the chest. It was a good thing that I didn't faint at the sight of blood or we would have really been in trouble! I knew we had to find where it was coming from and SOON.

I started checking him over and found out that it was coming from the catheter in his chest. The cap must have worked its way off during the night and the tubing was allowing the blood to flow back through the tubing and out the end. I was able to think fast enough to get the clamp shut on the tubing and that stopped the blood immediately. I crawled around on the floor to look for the cap, but I never found it. I had no idea what happened to it, but I was so thankful that we found the problem when we did. George could have easily bled to death.

I wanted to call an ambulance to take him to the hospital but he wasn't having any part of that idea. (Men and their pride!) I called the ER instead and the nurse said I had done the right thing but that I needed to bring him to the hospital and have the CVC checked. We already had an early appointment so we left as soon as I could get him dressed. (Yes, he walked to the car, and he walked into the hospital from the parking garage.)

The lab was our first stop. It was packed, and I mean *packed*. Every chair in the waiting room was full and people were standing in every spot that was available to stand in. I had never seen it that busy. George wasn't feeling all that great and I knew he wasn't up for all that time on his feet. I found a wheelchair, pushed it up behind him, and told him to sit. He gave me that look that said he wasn't "thrilled" about my ordering him around, but he sat down. I knew he was glad to have a place to sit, even if it *was* a wheelchair. I wasn't sure how much blood he had lost and I wasn't taking a chance on having to pick him up off the floor!

While we were waiting for our Fast Track appointment, I wheeled him into the infusion department. They took us back to a room and took a look at the problem with his CVC. I was right, somehow the end cap had worked its way off the end of the tubing. The nurse cleaned it and changed the bandages and replaced the cap that had been lost. She took some cultures from inside the tubing to have sent to the lab. They couldn't take a chance that bacteria had entered the tubing while the cap was off. The culture reports would be back the next day. I prayed that they would be negative.

At Fast Track, everything checked out OK. His platelets were low and the nurse told us that they had to come up

God is in the Details

before Thursday or his chemo would be delayed.

I knew that chemo needed to stay on schedule, but by this time, I was hoping for a little delay. George had been through so much already and I was constantly concerned that he was too weak for another round. We were both looking forward to having the last round over with, but I feared the ARA-C.

Back at the apartment, George informed me that the bone pain was starting again. I had an appointment with my surgeon to have my stitches removed and he wanted to go along with me; I thought he needed to stay home with the heating pad and take some pain pills! After going back and forth about it, he finally decided to take a nap and I left for my appointment.

I was so glad to be getting the bandages off and those stitches out. The first thing that I was going to want to do was "scratch" but I knew I didn't dare. I was hoping that once the stitches came out, the itch would leave!

The doctor was very happy with the way my nose looked. He said the skin graft had taken well and that he expected my nose to look great in a few months. "A few months?" He had never said anything about months; I was thinking more like weeks.

He kept going on and on about how well everything was healing and then he held the mirror out to me. I took one look and thought I was going to get sick. I wanted to cry, but I held it in. The doctor was so happy; "why wasn't I feeling that same enthusiasm?" I felt disfigured and wished that I hadn't looked in that mirror. He said he would see me back in one week for a follow-up, and that he was confident that everything was going ahead of schedule.

I walked to the elevator and once inside, the tears came. I couldn't hold them back a minute longer and I was glad that the elevator went down to the parking level without anyone else getting on. I didn't want to see anyone even though the

162

doctor had put a small bandage on my nose. I was in the throes of self-pity and I didn't want an audience.

All the way back to the apartment I talked to God. I recognized that this reaction was temporary but I didn't want George to see me so upset. I wasn't about to go home and cry on his shoulder about a scar on my face while he was just trying to survive. The scar on my face would eventually heal, and I knew that I just needed to get it together!

I was going to put on a brave front whether I felt brave or not.

The next morning was Wednesday, February 16. Buddy got me up about 6:00 for his first "tour" of the grounds and when we got back, George was still asleep. I decided this was a good time to clean my wound for the first time. I went into the bathroom, got my special soap ready along with some peroxide, some ointment, and a small bandage. I carefully took the old dressing off, gently washed the area, and used the peroxide. Next came the ointment, and finally the bandage. I was so proud of myself. I had gotten through all that a lot easier than I thought I would. Then it hit me. I broke out in a cold clammy sweat; I started to get sick to my stomach, and the next thing I knew I was lying on the bathroom floor. I had passed out!

I wasn't out for long, or at least I don't think I was. I called for George and lucky for me he heard me. He came into the bathroom and got me a cold, wet washcloth and helped me up off the floor. I had the feeling he wanted to laugh at me, but his better judgment took over and he kept quiet and helped me back to bed. I couldn't help but think that it was a darned good thing I didn't react in that way when I had to take care of him. My nursing skills would have been called into question for sure.

Eleven

· · ✿ · ·

Thursday, February 17. We had our appointment with Dr H to see if everything was a go for the last round of chemo. I took George by wheelchair and without any complaints this time. He was totally exhausted and still suffering from the bone pain. For the past twenty-four hours he had been having a lot of shortness of breath. The first thing I did, of course, was start worrying about his heart. Dr. H wasn't happy with his lab reports at all and told us that his platelet counts were way too low for chemo to start right away. "Thank you, God" was all I could say. I knew that George was in no condition to go through this round of chemo just then. Dr. H was going to have him return the next day for two units of blood and reassured us that the shortness of breath was because his blood was so low. (With all the blood he had lost, I wasn't surprised!) They checked him for congestive heart failure and said that was NOT the problem. I knew that the blood transfusion would help to relieve the fatigue and only wished that they had scheduled it for that same day.

We had an appointment for the transfusion at 4:00 on Friday. It was delayed; *late as usual* should have been their "motto." They finally got to George at 5:50, almost two hours late this time. The pharmacy refused to release two units of blood because the lab had checked his hemoglobin when we arrived and it wasn't low enough for two units of blood. (Whatever! Just give him one unit and let's get on with it!) George didn't feel good and my patience was all but gone by that time.

The transfusion itself took two hours to complete. We were both starving and I had been feeling like a limp rag ever since my surgery. While he was having the transfusion, I sat in the recliner next to his bed, propped my feet up, and listened to the most relaxing sound that I had heard in a while, "silence." It was wonderful. Everything lately seemed to be getting to me and all the weeks and months of the intense pace that we had kept had worn me down. I honestly didn't know how George kept up with any of it. If I was exhausted, how must he feel?

I was beginning to wonder if my depression was getting worse or if maybe I was just homesick. All I knew was that I wanted to be with my family and I wanted my husband back the way he used to be. Every time I looked at him he seemed weaker to me. I knew that he was really pushing himself to keep his positive outlook, and I admired him for that. I would never really know what went on in that mind of his, but I couldn't imagine that it was easy to look ahead without the fear of "what if."

The week passed so slowly. I continued to feel unmotivated, but George steadily improved, a little each day. The blood transfusion had done the trick and we would be back on track with the chemo any day now. I was beginning to realize that part of the way I had been feeling was the dread of something happening once he started that

God is in the Details

last treatment. I wasn't so afraid of the actual *infusion*, but more of the weeks afterward when his counts would fall. I was also fearing the "what if"! "What if he got sick like he did after the last round of ARA-C?" I knew only too well what we might be facing and all I wanted to do was forget about it for as long as I could.

We decided to take another little trip so George could dig through more "buried treasure" at his friend's place near College Station. He had missed out on that second trip that he had planned with Bret, so being the *wonderful* wife that I am, I agreed to drive once again. This time I wanted to spend the night in a motel and just get away from it all, even if it was just for one day and one night! I wanted to get as far away from hospitals and labs and sickness as I possibly could and I knew George felt the same way. We could pretend for just a little while.

Buddy and I dropped George off in "junkyard paradise" and then I went to find a motel. I picked up some take-out for lunch and when we got to the room, Bud and I shared it. He was content to lie in bed with me after we had walked over the entire surrounding area for at least forty-five minutes so he could sniff all those delicious new smells that he found so exciting. I settled down on the bed, opened my novel, and spent the afternoon in *fantasyland*. I was so relaxed by the time George got to the motel that I didn't even want anything for dinner. He had gone out to eat with his friend before he got there so all we did was watch TV and make an early night of it.

Wednesday morning we made one more stop before heading back to Houston and reality! George knew a man who lived in the area who had a small military museum on his property. His house was beautiful and the setting was like something out of *Gone With the Wind*. There was a pond in front of his house and giant trees surrounded the yard. The day was gorgeous and the temperature was 82 degrees. (Maybe I wasn't so anxious after all to head back to Michigan before the snow melted!) George spent a couple of hours exploring, and then we headed back home.

The final round of chemo was to start the next day. We were excited and could hardly believe that the day we had been waiting for was almost here. George was ready and more than a little anxious to see Dr H and get the "go ahead."

It was Thursday, February 24, and Dr H had given George the "thumbs up." Chemo was scheduled and all we had to do was wait for the orders to be written and we would be free to go home until a room was ready.

We waited for over two hours for those orders to be written, but they weren't; everything was backed up. We finally decided not to wait any longer and I told the receptionist we were going out for lunch and would then head home. When everything was ready, they could call us!

Comfort food was what we both needed so we headed to our favorite burger joint. We had discovered Southwell's by accident one day when we had gone to a different pharmacy than we normally went to. This place was in the same strip mall and it had been packed that day. We had always believed that you could tell how good the food was by the amount of cars in the parking lot, so we went in! That day was no exception, it was packed as usual. Most of the time we tried to eat healthy food, but those burgers and homemade fries were definitely NOT in that category! We ignored all the rules and weren't even going to try to justify our decision; we were just going to enjoy ourselves! When we got to the apartment I noticed the light on the answering machine flashing and when I checked the message it was to say that George's room was ready.

Chemo didn't start that night and was still on hold by the next morning. The pH level in his blood was too low and they wouldn't start the chemo until they got that

God is in the Details

under control. We had learned from day one that chemo never started on time. There was always a blood test before the infusion and if there was the slightest thing that was even a little "off" nothing happened until the problem was corrected. Regardless of the waiting, we were glad that they were rigid about the precautions they took. We wanted the very best care possible and we always knew that George got just that.

While we waited for chemo to begin, I went for another follow-up at Dr. Nelson's office. I saw his partner this time and he too was very impressed with how my nose looked; he told me that Dr. Nelson had done a remarkable job. He couldn't believe that it had been only two and a half weeks since the surgery and was amazed at how well I was healing. I was truly thankful that the healing was going so well, but I could hardly bear to look at myself in the mirror when I took the bandage off. I felt like I had an elephant sitting on my nose and was sure that everyone must be staring at me whenever I went out without that bandage. Oh, I know I was vain, but that is my personality! I wasn't sure if my nose would ever look normal again, although both doctors assured me that it would in time. They had already told me I would need to have another procedure done at a later time. They would do dermabrasion, which would actually "sand" my scar and even out the texture of the skin. I would make an appointment to have that done when George and I returned to Houston in a few months for his first follow-up; until then, I was stocking up on Band-Aids!

I left the office feeling sorry for myself again. I hated the feeling of self-pity but that's how I felt. I didn't want a big, ugly scar on my face and I hated wearing a bandage everywhere I went. I knew I was blessed that a scar was all I had, but trying to be thankful was really hard right then. I had so many bigger and more important things going on in my life and here I was, crying over a scar!

When I got back to the hospital, I got on the elevator to go up to George's room. When I stepped inside the elevator I came face to face with a woman who had no nose. If anyone would have told me that I was going to have this experience, I would have thought they were either a liar or delusional; but it *happened!* I had seen about everything there was to see since we had been at MD Anderson, but never anyone without a nose. Right across the middle of her face was a loose bandage where her nose should have been. I tried not to stare but I found it impossible to look away. I was relieved when the doors opened and I was able to step out of the elevator. I didn't know whether I was supposed to feel sorry for her or just ashamed of myself! I decided that she didn't need my pity, only my prayers; what I needed was to ask for forgiveness! I had been caught up in how I looked on the outside when really what I needed to be concerned about was how I *looked* on the inside. The healing that needed to be done in me had absolutely nothing to do with my nose.

It had turned cold and rainy in Houston and chemo had finally started. George was already running a slight temperature and all he felt like doing was sleep. He wasn't much company and I decided to go home and try to get something accomplished. I knew that this was going to be the hardest round of chemo on George's body and I wanted to be rested up and prepared for whatever happened in the following days. Dr H had cut back on the dose of the ARA-C but wanted George to finish the protocol as prescribed. When he said it was going to be rough, we had some idea what he meant, but we still weren't really prepared.

By Sunday, the fever was pretty high. It was fluctuating between 102 and 103. Dr. H was taking added precautions this time and had done some cultures to make sure it was from chemo and not an infection. He was adding an antibiotic as

God is in the Details

well in hopes that if this should be an infection they could head it off before it got too bad. George was told that he wouldn't be coming home the next day, even if the chemo was completed. He would have to wait for the cultures to come back and that would be Tuesday at the earliest. George was discouraged but I told him "Hang in there two more days, that's all that's left, just two more days!" With that I got a half-hearted smile and he went back to sleep!

I went home and cleaned that apartment like it had never been cleaned before. I thought that if I worked hard enough and fast enough I wouldn't have time to think about what was going on at the hospital. I called to check on things and then went back to cleaning. It helped! I completely wore myself out and when I went to bed I didn't have a thought in my head. I fell asleep the minute my head hit the pillow.

Monday, February 28; CHEMO WAS FINISHED. Praise God, it was over. There would be no more chemo infusions and if God granted us that miracle that we had been praying for, *George would be cancer-free*. I stood in that hospital room, staring at the bravest man I had ever known! *He was my champion*. I don't believe that anyone had ever gone through as much as George had in the last seven months with any more perseverance and determination than he had. He had fought more than one battle in the past year, and now he was going to be free of needles and chemo poles, catheters protruding from his chest, bags of poison dripping into his body, endless trips for lab work and Fast Track appointments. It was finally happening. There would be only a few more trips to the hospital during the next couple of weeks and if everything went well, we were going home very soon.

When Dr H came in to check on George, he told us he would be discharged the next day. *If this was a dream, I certainly didn't want anyone to wake me up!*

George's hemoglobin was only 7.2 the next morning so that meant he needed a blood transfusion before he could go home. The culture reports were back and there was no infection, so that was the good news for the day. It was evening before the discharge papers were signed and we were ready to leave the hospital. As we walked through those doors we were both on top of the world. If nothing else happened, this would be the last time George would be an inpatient in the hospital. We almost had to pinch ourselves to make sure this was really happening.

All I wanted to do now was start packing to go home. We had decided to mail some boxes as I got them packed so that we would be able to rent a smaller U-Haul for the trip home. I wasn't sure if that was possible because we had accumulated a lot of "extras" along the way. I kept packing though, and we kept taking those boxes to the post office. George had his last appointment with Dr H scheduled for March 21 and that was our goal...to have everything packed and ready to leave Houston on March 22!! It looked like we might just make it home for Easter after all. It had been raining again and was actually "cold" outside. I chuckled to myself and thought "God, you are preparing me for that nasty weather in Michigan!" In between packing, I started making phone calls and getting things arranged for our move. I had the car serviced and had new tires put on it. I was READY!

The first trip to the lab after chemo took place two days after George came home. His counts were already dropping but the hemoglobin was good after the two units of blood he had before he left the hospital. The fatigue had started again, but we were expecting a couple of weeks of recovery before things would start to look up again. I was going to make sure that he got plenty of rest so that nothing would stop us from leaving Houston just as soon as possible.

God is in the Details

Our family was getting so excited with the prospect of our coming home in just a week or two. I received the cutest e-mail from our granddaughter Elizabeth. She told me that she had gone into our house in Michigan with her dad to check on things, and she said it was dark and cold and it didn't "smell" like our house. She said that when I was home my house was always "happy" and smelled like food and dishwasher soap! I think I laughed about that for days afterward. I just loved what she said. You never know what memories you will leave behind and I was glad that I had made some happy ones for her. My packing was going well but my list of things that still needed to be done was growing.

I had to take my Durango into the dealer in Houston because I had a recall on the ball joints and I wanted to make sure they were checked before we started our trip home. The mechanic had a list of things that he said needed to be done to it in addition to the recall so I told them to go ahead with the repairs and I would leave the car for the day. I dropped it off at 7 a.m. and when I went back to pick it up at 4:30, they had done all the repairs to the tune of $725. Then they had the nerve to tell me that they didn't have time that day to do the work on the recall! I was furious. The ONLY reason I had taken it in was for the recall, not for the extras. We could have waited until we got home for those repairs but I was trying to save time and have it all done at once. The mechanic and I went round and round and finally I told him to get the service manager. When he came over to talk to me I was sure he could tell by my "body language" that I wasn't a happy customer! I voiced my opinion about what had taken place with my vehicle and after he ran out of excuses he told me they would pay for a rental car for me if I would bring the Durango back in on Monday. I really didn't have many options. George had appointments on Monday and experience had taught me that a run to

ER could happen without warning. I needed the ball joints replaced, so I accepted the offer of a rental car.

The next day was Saturday and we had labs and Fast Track again. We got a little bit of bad news; George's platelets were low and he needed a transfusion! He had been overly optimistic and got a little depressed when he heard the news. I tried to encourage him and reminded him that this was to be expected since this was round 6 and he had gotten the ARA-C again. I told him that after the transfusion he would feel so much better and that everything would start looking up again. He wasn't convinced and to be honest, neither was I, but I knew we couldn't get down about it. There were always those setbacks that we dreaded, but we were just so ready to have this over with.

March 6…George's sixty-seventh birthday! I knew this wasn't going to be a very good birthday, so I went about trying to put some cheer into his day. I planned to cook all his favorite things for dinner and had gotten a small cake for dessert. The day started going downhill around mid-day. He would ask me a question and then turn right around and repeat it. That was something out of the ordinary which had me a little concerned. As the day wore on, his mood got worse. Everything I said was wrong and he didn't hesitate to tell me about it! While I was cooking our meal, he kept telling me that I was making too much noise! I could do nothing right and I tried not to take it personally, but it was getting to me. He really hurt my feelings when he wouldn't eat the nice meal I had made especially for him. After all my preparation, he said he wasn't hungry and that nothing tasted good. He was quiet before bed and whenever I would say anything to him he was quick to tell me that he didn't feel like talking. I could tell just by looking at him that he had a fever. I went to get the thermometer to take his temperature; 101.7. That knot

God is in the Details

of fear had started deep inside of me, and I knew that this was all leading up to something.

I wanted to go to the ER; he wanted to go to bed. I tried to talk him into it and he got angry. The only choice I had was to call the ER and see what they had to say. The nurse told me that his temperature was close enough to 102 and with everything else that was going on with him, she told me not to wait, but to bring him in right away. I wanted him to go willingly and by the time I got off the phone he had resigned himself to going. I was surprised, then really worried. He wasn't fighting me on this any more so I knew he was sick! George would NOT be willing to go to the ER again if he thought he didn't have to.

We got there around 9:30 p.m. The doctor on duty told me he was going to admit him because he had seen his chart and knew his history. He wasn't going to wait around until something worse happened. It was 3 a.m. when he got to a room. Sleep wasn't even an option for me that night. I sat in a chair and prayed.

I had to take the Durango to the shop by 7. I felt like a limp noodle when I walked out of the hospital and once I dropped off the car, it took me over an hour to get all the paperwork done for the car rental and then I had to stop at the apartment to see about Buddy. The little guy was about frantic from spending the night alone and was beside himself with excitement when I walked in. I got him taken care of and then I called George. He sounded awful. He said he still hadn't gotten any sleep and his temperature was 102. The doctor had just been in and said that this wasn't "unusual" but we already *knew* that. We had both just gotten so carried away with our plans to go home that we had forgotten to slow down and let the recovery process happen.

By the next day, George's white blood cell count was .4, his neutrophils were 0, and he had no bone marrow function! His hemoglobin had dropped from 11.2 to 9.8 and more blood was ordered to have on stand-by. I would NEVER get used to all this.

George's temperature would come and go and his counts stayed at the very bottom of the chart. The doctor was loading him up on the antibiotics and had started giving him two Neupogen shots a day to see if that would get the counts to come up quicker. They were going to give him two units of blood that afternoon and I was counting on that to make a huge difference.

When I got home that evening, I talked to my cousin Alice. A friend of ours had just lost her husband to cancer and I wanted to see how she was doing. After that phone call, I got depressed. I wanted to be able to do something for her, but what could I do? I couldn't change the situation and I couldn't bring her husband back. Right now that was all she wanted, and no one could give that to her. That started me thinking about how close I had come to losing my own husband and now we may be facing the same thing again. I wasn't sure how much more George could take. He was so weak and he couldn't seem to get over one thing until something else knocked him down. That conversation had brought out all the fear that I had tried so hard to keep buried inside. I knew the devil would use this to ruin my testimony, and right then he had me in his grip.

I felt defeated until I started thinking about those past seven months and how God had taken me by the hand and led me through each day, how He had held me up when I wanted to fall, how He had shown me time and time again that He was there beside me. I thought back to that ER experience just a couple of months before when I had been desperate and had cried out to Him in my anguish. He had been FAITHFUL; God didn't want me to feel despair. He wanted me to live a life of gratitude and He was going to teach me how to do just that!

God is in the Details

By Friday George had already had a platelet transfusion and two units of blood. He was quiet and a bit withdrawn and his cough had started up again. It was almost as if he were having spasms in his lungs because once he started coughing there was no stopping it. It was much worse this time and I was certain it was a result of the ARA-C. He had no appetite and refused to eat a bite of anything. He wasn't in the mood to talk and all he wanted to do was lie there with his eyes closed. This brought back the horror of January, but I refused to cave in again. I allowed him to have his space and just reassured him that I was right there if he needed me.

Dr H hadn't been on hospital duty all week and I was a little upset about that. He knew George's history better than anyone and I always felt more comfortable when George was in his care. He had a way about him that could reassure George better than anyone else. I really wanted to talk to him and was hoping we would see him soon.

By Saturday, George's condition was still unchanged. One of the other lymphoma doctors made the rounds and he talked to us about his options; he told us he would give this another twenty-four hours and if nothing had improved, he was going to try a drug called Leukine. (This is another drug that is used to stimulate the production of white blood cells in the bone marrow.) I could tell by the way he talked that he didn't really want to use this drug. When I questioned him about it, all he would say was that he would make his decision whether to try it or not the next day. Before he left he cautioned us that if George's temperature were to go much higher they wouldn't be able to help him because his immune system was so compromised.

It was a night of anxious waiting. I spent most of it tossing and turning and depending on God. By Sunday morning we had only the slightest improvement, but *anything* at this point was good news. It's amazing how little it took to encourage us. The neutrophils were only .28 but at least they weren't 0 any more! (The normal range for an absolute neutrophil count is 1.5-8.0.) His white blood cell count was still .7 (normal range is 4.3-10.8), and his platelets were down to 31,000 (normal is 140,000-390,000). Maybe some people wouldn't see this as any improvement at all, but I did. I knew that things weren't going to change overnight, but I clung to the hope that we would start to see things going in the right direction, possibly even hour by hour! I wasn't about to give up and neither was George. There was a reason why those little neutrophils had increased, even ever so slightly, and that was proof enough for me that something in his bone marrow was starting to work! The decision was made not to try the Leukine at this point and the doctor was going to see how things went in another twenty-four hours.

On Monday, those same little neutrophils had made their way up to .46. The white blood cell count was now .9. We were seeing only tiny improvements but *improvements* they were. George was scheduled to see Dr H in his office on March 21, and I knew there was no way that he would be able to keep that appointment. This was only the fourteenth but I decided to reschedule. He had to have CT scans, x-rays, and scopes done before that appointment and there was just NO WAY he would be able to do all that. He had been in the hospital for nine days already and I knew that even if he were to come home the next day, he would be in no condition to go through anything more than perhaps the scans.

I called Dr H's office and spoke with his assistant, Amy. She was shocked to hear that George was in the hospital. As it turned out, Dr H was out of the country and that's why we hadn't seen him. Amy and I discussed the tests that George was to have and she agreed that we should hold off

God is in the Details

on having the scopes done until we returned to Houston for his first follow-up. She told me that they wouldn't be able to do those now anyway because his platelet count was too low and they wouldn't do procedures like that until those counts returned to normal. She did suggest that we go ahead and arrange to have the CT scans done just as soon as George was able. I was relieved. I really didn't want him to have to do one more thing that would require any strain on his body. He had been practically at death's door twice in as many months, and I knew that this recovery was going to take quite a while.

The following day, he was able to come home. The lymphoma team really wanted him to stay in the hospital a few more days, but he practically begged them to let him come home. They finally agreed, but with strict limitations. He was to go absolutely nowhere except to the lab and Fast Track in a couple of days, and he had to keep his mask on unless he was inside the apartment. No one was to come in the apartment but me and it was imperative that we keep his exposure to other people at the barest minimum. He would have agreed to anything just to get out of that hospital!

When we got home, I got him settled in his favorite spot, on his recliner, and we talked about our plan to go home. He was so weak, I couldn't imagine that he was going to feel up to making a twelve-hundred-mile trip home anytime soon, but he was determined that we were going to leave Houston as soon as he saw the doctor. That was only a week away, and I really had my doubts. I wasn't going to say anything to discourage him, so I just kept packing things that I thought we wouldn't need before we left, and stacked the boxes wherever I could find room. I was going to call Hoffer's, the place where we had rented the furniture, and make arrangements for them to pick it up. I also needed to make a plane reservation for our son.

He was flying to Houston to drive us home. He knew the trip home was going to be very stressful on George and he didn't want me to have to do all the driving myself. I took another look at George and decided that I had better wait a couple of more days before making those calls. I just had a feeling that things weren't going to go as smoothly as he was hoping.

He woke up coughing at six the next morning. I made him some hot tea; next he tried cold Gatorade. He couldn't stop coughing. After taking a couple of big doses of cough medicine he quieted down enough to doze off. When he woke up again, he said he was cold. I got the thermometer and took his temperature; it was only 96.9. I felt a rush of relief...until the chills started. He was shaking so bad that I couldn't even get his clothes on him. I had already decided that we were going to the ER and there was no talking me out of it this time. I knew that I wasn't able to get him to the car by myself so I ran down the hall to get our neighbor Brad. Between the two of us we got him to the car.

For once the ER was empty, at least in the waiting room. We got a room in less than five minutes and when the nurse checked his temperature it was only 98.1. I was a bit puzzled but I knew that those violent chills and shaking were leading up to something. It took both me and the nurse to get his clothes off and by the time she took his vitals and rechecked his temperature, it was 104.7!

I felt like I was in an instant replay. I had been here before, more than once, and I really didn't understand what had happened this time. I knew that George had left the hospital too soon, but his temperature had been normal, his counts were inching up, and he had been given FOUR antibiotics. Even the ER doctor was puzzled. He had already told us that George would be admitted just as soon as they had a room available and until then, he would continue running tests.

God is in the Details

There I sat in the ER asking God to give me something to hang onto. I emptied myself out to Him and asked Him to fill me with his peace. I prayed for His healing touch once more for George and I could feel His love surround me. Just like the last time, He spoke to me with words from scripture and verses from hymns.

George had been given a shot of Demerol for the shaking and that had put him to sleep. I went outside to make a call to our pastor back home. My hands were shaking so hard that I could hardly hold the phone to my ear. There was the fear that this could be septic shock and I knew that could be devastating. I knew that George needed extra prayers and I knew that my pastor would make sure he got them. I knew he would send out a special prayer request to our church family and I could rest, knowing that God was hearing those prayers.

A room was available around 3:30 and George was moved to the ninth floor to the lymphoma section. When the doctor came in to see him, he told us that George had pneumonia. I couldn't comprehend how that could be possible! He had just finished four intravenous antibiotics and he was standing there telling us that this was pneumonia! I didn't doubt that they had "named" it pneumonia, but I KNEW it was from the ARA-C. Nothing else made a bit of sense to me. All I kept thinking about was Jay and his diagnosis of pulmonary fibrosis! For a brief moment I started fearing that George was heading in that same direction. I decided that thinking beyond the present wasn't going to help either of us, so I tried to put that thought out of my mind.

When I got to the hospital the next morning, they were just getting ready to give George a transfusion. I had lost track of how many he had already had in the past two months, but I no longer feared them. I welcomed them because I knew he would improve and would start feeling a lot better in no time. His counts were still climbing, which was great news. The white blood cell count was up to 4.2 and the neutrophils were 3.53! Both were on the low side of normal, but this was progress! The doctor told me that they were giving him a huge dose of antibiotics and hoped to see some major improvement in the next couple of days.

Packing was still underway whenever I wasn't at the hospital. There was no stopping me...I was determined that everything would be in boxes and ready to go the very minute the doctor said we could leave for home. I knew that this meant everything to George, and of course, I couldn't wait! Our plans to be home for Easter had to change, but now none of those plans really mattered. As much as I had wanted to be home by then, my ONLY desire right then was to have George home with me, even if it was in our "home" in Houston!

There were times that I would get that cold feeling of dread deep down in the pit of my stomach; I would start to question whether we had done the right thing after all by making the decision to go ahead with this type of chemo. I believe that is a normal fear. I believe that all of us second guess our decisions at one point or another, but it all still came back to this: God had led us to MD Anderson. I would never doubt that. God had prepared this journey for us, had walked this path ahead of us to prepare our way. No matter what my fears had been, God had given me peace. I continued on with my packing and my plans and decided to leave the rest to God. After all, *He was the one in charge.*

Five days after he was admitted to the hospital, George got to come home. He walked out of there looking like he had been in a war, and he had! He had been in this war for almost a year and I was so ready for the battle to end. They had done CT scans before they discharged him and now all we had to do was see Dr H for the last time; then we would be free to go home!

Twelve

·· ᏬᎶᎽᎧ ··

The same day George came home from the hospital, we got wonderful news from home! Our Cathy was pregnant! She had been trying for so long to conceive and it had finally happened. I was floating on air! George was home and we were going to have a new little grandchild in November! What a blessing! Things had certainly started looking up for the Pretty family. I was ready to start making those final plans for our departure and if things worked out, we could be leaving in a week!

Tuesday, March 22. This was turning out to be another bad day. It seemed as though we would have one terrific day, and then turn around only to be hit with yet another problem. I had been looking forward to a stress-free day; no hospitals, no doctors, no labs. George was still in bed and I was hoping that was a good sign that he was getting some much needed rest. When I opened the bedroom door to check on him, I found him awake. He said he had been awake for a while, but just didn't feel like getting up. I walked over to the bed, and rubbed my hand across his head. (That was a habit that I had acquired since I was always looking for signs of a fever.) I was expecting a cool brow, but what I felt was a forehead that was burning up with fever! I couldn't believe it. I picked up the thermometer which by now had found a "home" in the drawer of the nightstand, 102.8!! This wasn't happening; I just could NOT believe this was happening. How could his temp be normal for two days and then spike to over 102 without warning? There was nothing else to do but get him dressed and back to ER.

Neither of us spoke a word once we got to the car. What could there possibly be to say at that point? We both knew that this was going to call for another hospital admission and neither of us wanted to discuss it. It was as though we were trapped in a time warp and couldn't get out of it. The same thing just kept happening and neither of us could do a thing about it except go along with it.

We got to the ER at 10:45 and into a room on the tenth floor at 6:30 in the evening. The whole staff of doctors were as surprised as we were. They talked about doing a bronchoscope to check his lungs and decided to call in a doctor from infectious disease for a consultation. As soon as they started an IV and got some antibiotic going, the fever went down. I was so frustrated with everything and everyone. I didn't understand why, if this was an infection, that the antibiotics weren't working! Everything was fine as long as he was on the medications, and once they stopped them, he was sick within twenty-four hours. I knew only too well that these medications could cause serious problems with an already compromised immune system, but what choice did they have? They had to try to find a cause and treat it the best way they knew how.

I was beyond the point of exhaustion and I couldn't even imagine how George must have felt. By now he had

God is in the Details

to really be ready to give up. I had no answer, the doctors had no answer, and we all just seemed to be going through the motions. George wouldn't talk, I didn't want to talk, and even the doctors didn't want to talk. All we could do was wait. Home seemed very far away. All our plans were once again on hold, and I had no idea what to do next.

We were both a bit more optimistic by the next morning. We had a visit from the infectious disease specialist and he told us he would be studying all of George's lab reports and would get back with us by afternoon. He suspected a viral infection that would require a different type of medication. If it turned out to be a different strain of bacteria than the ones they had been treating, then a change of medication would be called for in that case as well. The one bright spot this time was the fact that George wasn't neutropenic; his counts were all good and his own body could fight whatever infection this was with a little help from medication. That was a HUGE weight that was lifted.

George and I made a decision. We were going home next week if he was able to travel. If he wasn't able to go by car, then he would fly. Either way, we were going home. If this new approach worked, all the better, but if not, we would find a doctor in Michigan to treat him. He wasn't going to go through another hospital admission in Houston. He had had enough and so had I. We needed to be home where I had help and both of us had the support of family and friends. We had both reached our limit and now it was time to pray for the strength to get home!

When the doctor came back to tell us how he planned to treat the infection he explained that the antibiotic that George had been receiving was called Vancomycin and was used in treating the type of pneumonia that George had. This infection happened in immunocompromised individuals like George who had undergone chemotherapy. The bacteria were resistant to multiple antibiotics and unfortunately the Vancomycin wasn't working. They had another drug that was used as a last resort and would be starting that drug immediately. If he was still improving and had no fever, he was to be discharged the next day.

It was now March 25. Excluding the two nights that he had been home between hospital admissions, George had been in that hospital for a total of twenty days since he had finished his chemo! I had been up most of the night with a sinus headache and my whole body was a mass of aches and pains. (Exhaustion does that!) I managed to get George home before noon and then went to the pharmacy to get the new prescription of Zyvox filled. This was the new medication that they had put him on and he was to stay on it for at least two weeks. I had NO idea how much that one prescription was going to cost, so I about fainted when the pharmacist said $1245.00. (We had no prescription insurance!) I hated to tell George how much that little trip cost us; the shock might have sent him back to the ER! When I got back to the apartment we had just enough time for a quick lunch and then we were off to see Dr H. This was to be our last appointment with him before we left Houston and it was the day we had waited for. It had been nine months since the first time we saw him, and now this was the day he would tell us if George had achieved a remission!

It was Good Friday! It was one year to the day since George had been diagnosed!

We walked into that office holding hands, just like we had all those months ago. We had been afraid to hear what he had to say back then, but today we were excited! We already knew that the news was going to be good, but we needed to hear it spoken out loud. Dr H and his assistant Amy walked in together, both with a huge grin on their face. Dr H reached out his hand and shook mine and then turned to George and took his hand and said to him, *"You*

God is in the Details

have had a complete response to the chemo!" The news was the very best that we could have had. There was no evidence of any active lymphoma and the lymph nodes were now normal size. That small room could barely contain all the excitement and enthusiasm that we were sharing. Dr H went on the say that he expected George to continue to do well and that he wanted to see us back in Houston in three to four months for follow-up testing. They would carefully watch for any signs of a relapse for the next five years and would re-test him about four times a year for the first couple of years; then would spread those check-ups out to twice a year if nothing had changed. After another round of hand shakes and hugs, we were FREE. Dr H didn't hesitate to say that we could leave for home as soon as George felt up to making the trip. He did suggest that we phone our regular doctor so that he could be seen once we got home to make sure that his counts were still increasing. Our feet never touched the ground all the way to the parking garage. We were filled with gratitude for the doctors who took such amazing care of George through his heart surgery and chemo, but we knew who the *real* "physician" was! *God had given us our miracle.*

Cathy called once to say that she had a craving for olives. The next time she called she was suffering from heartburn! I laughed at her and the new pregnancy sensations. I told her, "Get used to it; you have a long way to go." She was so happy and so was I. The timing seemed so right. We were on our way home and I would be there for the whole pregnancy. I didn't want to miss a single part of it.

The weekend went by in a blur. I finished the last of the packing and had made all the necessary phone calls to have the furniture picked up, the utilities turned off, and reservations made for our son's flight. All that was left to do was pick up the U-Haul. In the middle of all my arrangements Cathy called again. This time they had gone out for dinner and she had eaten Chinese. She always loved snow peas but she took one bite and was instantly nauseated. She said she would never eat another snow pea as long as she lived. I told her that pregnancy was a time of opposite extremes for sure and that she had yet to see the worst of it.

Something she said caused that ever present alarm bell in me to go off. She was having some mild cramping and had called her OB. He told her that was probably normal for early pregnancy but to keep a watch on it and if it became more than just mild cramping she should go to ER. She called me again a couple of hours later to say that she was having sharp pains in her right side and was getting scared. She wanted to know what I thought. I wanted to reassure her so I told her to give it a bit more time and maybe the pains would stop. About twenty minutes later she called back, crying. She was on her way to the ER. When she had gotten home she noticed that she was bleeding and called her doctor back. He told her to go straight to the hospital.

My face felt like it was on fire. I was instantly in my panic mode. "Please, God, take care of my babies." I knew this wasn't good. I had had three kids and I had never had anything like that happen. I tried to tell myself that every woman is different and that this didn't necessarily mean that she was going to miscarry. She called when she left the ER to say that they had released her because the pains had stopped and the blood tests they did showed that everything looked OK. I didn't sleep much and just kept thinking of how sad and disappointed she would be if she lost her baby.

Easter morning! HE IS RISEN. How we had wanted to be home and in church that morning! It wasn't meant to be. God had His plan and that's the one that mattered. We were disappointed but just the thought of celebrating next year, cancer-free, was our reward! I got out of bed

God is in the Details

wanting some fresh Krispy Kreme donuts so I threw on some clothes and started out the door. Sitting out in the hall, right in front of our door, was a pot of beautiful spring tulips. Attached was a small balloon that said "Happy Easter." It was from our neighbors, Millie, Gordon, and their little girl Carson. What a wonderful surprise! Just the night before, we had gotten a jigsaw puzzle of the Lord's Supper from Brad and Judi along with a doggie bag of treats for Buddy from Radar. We had great neighbors that had become dear friends.

After we had our coffee and freshly made donuts (YUM) I decided to call Cathy. She was feeling so much better and the bleeding and cramping had stopped. Her mood was greatly improved and I could hear the relief and happiness in her voice. I got a burst of energy after that phone call and decided to tackle the last of the packing job that I had been dreading.

We had to take the computer apart and pack it carefully in the boxes we had brought it in. George said he would do that for me and even though I argued with him that he should be resting, he did it anyway. He was totally exhausted when that was done but insisted that he would disassemble the small desk that I had bought to put the computer on. Just looking around the apartment I was beginning to get nervous wondering if everything was going to fit into the U-Haul. I talked it over with George and he thought I was *nuts* to think all this stuff was going to fit. I decided to call U-Haul the next day to see if they had a size larger available. I couldn't think of anything worse than packing it full only to find that I still had boxes that wouldn't fit. I had to call around to a few places before I found one that had the size I needed.

George had one final visit to the hospital on Monday to have his CVC removed. This was the day he had been anticipating for a long time. He said once that came out he could finally believe that the ordeal was really behind him. He said he felt "untethered." I laughed at the analogy, but I could understand how he must have felt. After we left the hospital we took the cable box back to Time Warner and then went to the Residence Inn to check in. Hoffer's was coming to pick up our rental furniture that afternoon and we would need a place to sleep that night. We had everything arranged and all we had to do was go back to the apartment to wait for the guys to come for the furniture. While we waited I tried to call Cathy. I hadn't heard from her all day and was beginning to worry about her. It wasn't like her to "disappear" and not let me know where I could reach her. She didn't answer her home phone or her cell phone. I didn't have her work phone number because I had packed my address book in one of the boxes. I tried to push the worry out of my mind, and kept myself busy.

Once the furniture had been picked up, there was no place for us to sit. The TV didn't work because we had returned the cable box, so we headed to the Residence Inn.

I ordered some take-out for dinner and after we ate I tried calling Cathy again. This time Scott answered the phone. He said he was just about to call me to tell me that Cathy was in the hospital. The pains had returned, this time so severe that they had doubled her over while she was at work and she had to call Scott to take her to the hospital. They still weren't sure what was going to happen with the baby, but were keeping her overnight for observation. He gave me the number of the hospital and I tried calling her but she wasn't in a regular room so they transferred me to a nurse in the ER area. She told me that Cathy was having tests but would tell her that I had called.

George was exhausted. He had had a long day and wasn't used to being on his feet quite so much. I felt bad, dragging him around all day, but he insisted that he needed to try to get some of his strength back and refused to lie down and rest. He

God is in the Details

said he had been in bed too long already and was tired of it. That must have changed though, for as soon as he finally did lie down, he was out like a light. Buddy was trying his best to understand what was going on. First all the furniture had disappeared, and now he was sitting next to me in another strange place. He just took things in stride; sometimes I thought he did a lot better job of that than I did.

It was late, but I finally reached Cathy. She was losing hope fast. The doctors were afraid that she may have an ectopic pregnancy and as soon as they could be sure about it, she would have to have surgery. Her heart was broken and so was mine. I tried praying. I told God that I trusted His perfect judgment. I asked Him to forgive us for being so fragile, but I knew He understood. I knew that this little life had been formed in Cathy's womb by His hand. This was His creation and He was the one who would decide what happened. My comfort came in knowing that this little life already had a soul and that if God should decide that it wasn't to be born, then it would be with Him in heaven.

Tuesday morning I called Cathy. She still wasn't sure what was happening and promised to call me the minute she saw the doctor. George and I had breakfast and then went to get the U-Haul. We had hired some guys to load it for us, so we met them at the apartment. Before they even arrived, Cathy called to say they were taking her to surgery. They had confirmed that this was definitely a pregnancy in her tube and she was in danger of it rupturing. I have never wanted to be with anyone as much as I wanted to be with her at that moment. I knew that Scott was with her, but I also knew that she needed her mother. She had waited so long to have a child, and now that child was lost to her. If only we had been home…I stopped that thought almost as fast as it came to my mind. I was where God wanted me and Scott was with Cathy. It was his baby just as much as it was hers, and they needed to go through this together. I would be there for her when she needed me the most, after it was all over.

The U-Haul was loaded and we had said our good-byes to our neighbors. We got to the Residence Inn just before James arrived. I hadn't seen him in eight months and he looked wonderful to a mother's eye. This was the first time he had seen his dad bald and that was the first thing he teased him about. It was wonderful to have him with us. I felt as though it would take us forever to make up for all the time we had spent apart. We ordered supper and the guys talked; I waited to hear from Scott.

He finally called me to say that everything had gone well in surgery but that the tube was bleeding into the abdominal cavity and it had turned into a life-threatening situation. They had been able to do the surgery with the laparoscope so that would make the recovery a lot easier. Since Cathy now had only one functioning tube, that would cut her chances of getting pregnant again in half. She had already gone through so much with infertility; this really was going to be hard for her to hear. She was still in recovery and Scott hadn't been able to tell her any of this yet. I wanted to ask God "Why?" Instead, I thanked him for saving my daughter's life and then I asked Him to give her another baby some day.

At precisely 7:30 a.m. on March 30, we left Houston. We were going HOME. There had been many dark days for us in Houston, but God had brought us to where we were that day. George had faced death more than once, and I had seen God perform more miracles in my life than I had ever thought possible.

Epilogue

·· ❧ ··

We woke up in our own bed on April Fool's Day, 2005. It wasn't a dream and it wasn't an April Fool's joke, it was the real deal...WE WERE HOME!

I hated to give up the warm comfort of the bed but I knew that Buddy needed to go out. When I opened the back door he sat down to wait for me to put his leash on. He hadn't realized it yet, but he had a huge backyard to run around in and I didn't have to go with him! He wasn't sure at first what I expected him to do so I walked out on the deck and called him. It didn't take long until he was running around the yard with his ears flying! It was the first time he had been free to run in a long time and I could already see that he was as happy to be home as I was.

George woke up with the same excitement I was feeling. The trip had been hard on him, but he never uttered one word of complaint! He was just happy to be on his way home.

I went to the kitchen to put on a pot of coffee and stopped in my tracks when I opened the cabinet door; a family of

God is in the Details

mice had taken up residence while we were gone. The more I investigated the worse it got. This was more than a family of mice, it was a whole neighborhood. I could see that this would be the first job I would have to tackle.

We decided to get dressed and go out for breakfast. There was NO way I was going to do anything in that kitchen until I had eaten a good meal and had armed myself with cleaning supplies and at least a dozen mouse traps.

Later in the day, the kids began arriving; we were having our own little family reunion! I was especially happy to see Cathy. I knew that she needed her family around her to support her and she was in need of a big dose of love from her mom. I had plenty of that to give!

Having the kids with me was the greatest joy I had felt since George was told he was in remission. I couldn't seem to get enough of them and it seemed that we had been apart forever. I laughed more that day than I had laughed in the past year. All I wanted at that moment was to have things stay like that forever.

The guys unloaded the U-Haul and when they left I had a family room stacked with boxes. I just looked at all those boxes and smiled. I didn't care how long it took me to unpack, I just knew that I wasn't going to pack or unpack another box for a very long time. I walked from room to room with tears rolling down my cheeks. This was what perfect contentment felt like and I thanked God once more for bringing us home.

Our first Sunday home we went to church. George was still very weak and still on a very strong antibiotic, but I don't think a team of horses would have kept him from church that day. Everyone knew that we were home and were waiting for us when we got there. It was like another homecoming all over again. I had no words to describe the outpouring of love we received from our church family. They had supported us for the nine months we were in

Diane Pretty

Houston by sending cards, letters, gifts, e-mails, and most importantly, by their ceaseless prayers on our behalf. There were more hugs that morning than I could count and why I bothered putting on my makeup that morning I will never know. I had cried it all off before the church service had even begun.

Spring had come to Michigan and I was able to enjoy our new yard that had been in such a mess the year before. All my new flower beds were beginning to come alive in every shade of color imaginable. It was beautiful! Life was good once again.

George's energy level was improving at about the same rate at his new hair was appearing. His skin was now a healthy pink instead of the gray pallor of chemo days and his attitude was always positive. Anytime someone would ask how he was doing, his answer would always be, "I'm cured until further notice!"

When we had been home only a couple of weeks, I got some disturbing news from Cathy. She had just gotten home from the hospital. She had continued to have problems ever since her surgery and Scott had taken her to the ER with severe cramping and bleeding. An ultrasound had shown a fetus in her uterus; it was the twin of the baby she had just lost. The doctor told her that this was rare and called it a heterotopic pregnancy. One fertilized egg had made it to the uterus and implanted while another one had become trapped in her fallopian tube. The chances of the second fetus surviving were less than 30 percent and it appeared that she was already starting to miscarry. I didn't know what to say to her. She was about to lose her second baby in less than three weeks. Sometimes we are allowed to see the reason for our pain, but other times we simply have to believe that God knows best.

George and I went to Houston at the end of June for a week of testing. It was a great week with the exception of

God is in the Details

a couple of days of "prep" before his colonoscopy, but it was worth it when he was once again given the "all clear" verdict. We met Brad and Judi for dinner one night while we were there and when it was time to leave, I felt really sad. I had some wonderful times in Houston and I would always feel like that was a time of rebirth for me.

We had a scare that first Thanksgiving after we were home. George woke up one morning with a fever. He said he just felt so tired and didn't want to get out of bed. That brought back all those memories of the times in Houston when a fever meant the beginning of ER visits and hospital admissions.

The kids had been at our place for Thanksgiving and Scott and Cathy had spent the night with us. Scott helped me get George into the car and Cathy rode to the hospital with us. When we got to the ER they took blood tests and x-rays. While we waited, his temperature kept climbing. The ER doctor had called our family doctor, Dr. Lisa Booth, and together they decided to admit him.

When Dr. Booth came in to see him she told us that his WBC count was pretty low but nothing had showed up on the x-ray. George pointed out a sore that he had on his thigh and asked her to check it. She said it looked like a staph infection so she decided to do a biopsy to make sure. Just in case, she started him on IV medication to cover that possibility. Her main concern was the fear that his lymphoma had come back. His WBC count was only 1.7 and I knew that spelled trouble. I refused to believe that his lymphoma was back and that his remission had only lasted for nine months after all he had gone through.

The next morning, Dr. Booth came in to say that George did have a staph infection and by that time, two more lesions had appeared. She said this could possibly be the cause of his problem, but she wanted to transfer him to a larger hospital and place him in the care of an oncologist.

Diane Pretty

She allowed me to take him by car to Kalamazoo and we arrived there about 6 p.m.

George was very sick but we knew that we wouldn't find out anything more until the next morning. He finally got settled into bed and I spent most of the night in prayer. I knew where my strength would come from and I wanted to be filled with God's grace for what we might hear the following morning.

We met with the oncologist, Dr. Liepman, early the next morning and she was as puzzled about this situation as we were. George had just had CT scans done the previous month and everything had been OK. She couldn't understand why things would have changed so suddenly. She told us she would do a bone marrow aspiration to see if the lymphoma was back. Everything seemed to be pointing to that and this doctor wasn't encouraging at all. In fact, she said that it appeared that George's lymphoma was back with a vengeance!

We wouldn't know anything definite for days and the wait was going to be very difficult. I knew there was hope, but sometimes it was so hard to find that hope in the midst of tears and pain. I knew that we had been through this before and that God was still very much in control.

George was so sick that he started telling me he didn't care to live like this anymore. If the lymphoma had returned he didn't want to continue the fight. I knew he was terribly ill but I didn't want him to give up. I said, "Losing people that I love is really hard on me so I hope you aren't planning to die!" All he would say to that was, "I'm not making plans in that direction, but if I get worse I don't want to live." In all those months in Houston he had never once said anything about wanting to give up.

It had been a full week and his temperature was still 102. I didn't want to lose that thin strand of hope that I was clinging to but I was getting more worried by the

God is in the Details

day. George had been so convinced that he was "cured" and now he was starting to have doubts whether he should have gone through all that chemo or not. I reminded him that God had directed us to Houston and this wasn't the time to start second guessing God's plan for us. Then I reminded him of his heart surgery and how he might have died from a heart attack if it weren't for the chemo causing symptoms. I could still clearly see how God's hand was in all this, but George had lost his will to keep fighting. I wanted him to get his determination back; I wanted to see that same fight in him that he had had for over a year and a half. I wanted the George I knew to wake up and get well.

Things got worse before they got better. One day he told me that we had to start making arrangements. I asked, "Arrangements for what?" "For my funeral," he said. I wasn't even going to "go there." I refused to even talk about anything to do with death or funerals. I knew that something had to happen and happen FAST, because I was at the end of my endurance.

That night before I went to bed, I told God that I was putting George completely in His hands. I wasn't able to keep on encouraging him when I felt so discouraged myself. I prayed that He would be merciful and heal George, but I promised Him my faith and total trust no matter what He was about to do in my life. God deserved my all and I committed everything to him that night. I felt totally empty and there was nothing left for me to say, nothing else for me to ask for. God knew it all and His will would be done. I had accepted that.

On Friday December 2, we received the news that the bone marrow was clear! *The lymphoma had not recurred.* His WBC count was up to 3.0. Do I believe in miracles? Oh yeah!!! The next day the WBC count was 5.1. On Monday, December 5, George walked out of the hospital for the last time.

Every check-up has brought nothing but good news for us. George has gone on with his life and for the most part does everything he wants to do. Soon he will have reached three years of remission and, God willing, he will celebrate his seventieth birthday in just a few months.

Our friend Norm continues to remain in remission as well. Jay does have fibrosis in his lungs and his doctors say that he is a miracle. (See, Jay, I asked God for your miracle and He granted it!) He continues to enjoy life and he and his wife, Linda, travel Europe every chance they get.

Bridget's husband, Charles, has already passed the three-year mark in his remission and they are waiting to adopt a baby from China.

Our daughter Rose is doing well. She had undergone more surgery but continues to live life. She is still remarkable.

Yes, my ugly nose finally healed just as the doctors promised and with a little makeup no one ever notices my scar.

Buddy was so lonesome in that big yard of his that George and I took pity on him. Against our better judgment, I went in search of a playmate for him. It turned out to be a great decision and he and "Maggie" are inseparable.

We were sad for a long time about those little twin "angels" that were lost, but God will heal our hearts if we allow Him to. "He also gives us the desires of our hearts!" On October 26, 2006, Cathy gave birth to our grandson, Brayden Thomas Hoag, weighing in at seven pounds, eight ounces. This proud grandmother was there to welcome him when he took his first breath.

I could write another book about what God has done in my life, but how could I ever find the words to explain how that time in Houston became the best time of my life?

God is in the Details

Nothing before or since has touched my heart in quite the same way as sharing that journey with my husband. I discovered my strengths as well as my weaknesses but most of all I discovered who I could become when I allowed God to mold me into the person He wanted me to be.

I want to leave you with these thoughts:

"If you belong to Jesus, you can do almost anything!"

"The closer you walk to Jesus, the easier your journey will be."

"Prayer changes things!"

"God is God, and we're not, and that's OK!"

"If you are a Christian you have HOPE, and no matter how difficult your struggle, remember one thing, "GOD IS IN THE DETAILS."

ISBN 142515264-3